Interview Extracts

When Pat Adair was pregnant for the third time, her husband would pat her stomach and ask, "How's Sharon's kid?"

Mrs. Adair said she had no problem handing the baby she gave birth to over to the couple from Philadelphia she had it for. "I was the only way these people could have a child," she said. "It wasn't like giving a child up for adoption. It was their baby. I was simply having it.

I have never thought of myself as the mother. It isn't having a child that makes you a mother, it's raising the child."

After 10 futile years of trying to become pregnant, the woman in the Philadelphia birthing room was overwhelmed. A mother at last, she clamped the umbilical cord and clutched the infant to her bosom. "To see my son being born was the greatest thing that ever happened to me. That was the closest I will come to having a baby," she said.

For it was another woman who lay on the table, exhausted from childbirth. The mother was Pat Adair, a surrogate hired to have the baby. "I was just a carrier. I was carrying the baby for her," Mrs. Adair said. "From the day I conceived, it was her baby. She was the mother right from the beginning. I was never the mother. I never felt the baby was mine. They handed the baby right to her and her husband. If you could have seen the look on their faces, how happy they were, there's no way I could have kept it."

A SURROGATE TELLS HER STORY

A SURROGATE MOTHER'S STORY

PATRICIA ADAIR

PaperJacks LTD.

TORONTO   NEW YORK

PaperJacks

A SURROGATE MOTHER'S STORY

PaperJacks LTD.

330 STEELCASE RD. E., MARKHAM, ONT. L3R 2M1
210 FIFTH AVE., NEW YORK, N.Y. 10010

Originally published in hardcover edition
by Loiry Publishing House Inc. 1987

PaperJacks edition published November 1988

10 9 8 7 6 5 4 3 2 1

ISBN 0-7701-0994-2

Contents

1. My Decision 11
2. Delay 21
3. The Program 29
4. Family And Friends 37
5. Getting Chosen 45
6. The Contract 57
7. Insemination 67
8. Meeting The Father 77
9. Meeting Sharon 93
10. A Live Radio Talk Show 105
11. People's Comments 123
12. Live Television Show 133
13. Our Doubts 141
14. Hospital Policy 149
15. Losing My Job 155
16. Other Surrogate Mothers 163
17. Starting A New Job 173
18. The Last Weeks 181
19. The Birth 191
20. Hospital Stay 203
21. Saying Goodbye 215
22. Moving On 223
23. Contract Disputes 239
24. One Year Later 249
25. From Family And Friends 255
26. Four Years Later 267

To a very special friend ...
Sharon

And to my husband John and my three
sons John, Michael, and Mark ...
I Love You

A Letter From Sharon

From the time I received a telephone call from Patty saying I was going to become a mother, I felt just like the mother-to-be. From the first moment of my son's birth, I *was* a mother.

We were very fortunate to have Patty as our Surrogate Mother. She took me step-by-step through the pregnancy and we always kept in touch. If I didn't get a letter from her, I would get a phone call. I knew exactly how she was feeling and what the doctor had to say.

Patty and I met a few times at the mall and it was always like meeting a good friend that I had known all my life. I never had a problem talking to her about anything and we always enjoyed the time we spent together.

I remember the last time I saw her at the mall, before the baby was born. She was a sight! She is a beautiful woman—even at that time, when she looked like she was carrying around a basketball under her clothes. That day at the mall, I bought a teddy bear planter for my baby's room. I was really excited. I was talking about decorating the nursery and about naming the baby, and Patty was just as comfortable to be talking about all that with me. I know some people will never understand how we could be so close. Patty and I became friends because we genuinely liked each other.

Waiting for the baby to come made June of 1984 a tough month. I don't think I hardly slept until the baby was born. My husband would wake up at 1:30 a.m. because of the noise I was making while running the sweeper, changing kitchen curtains, or doing the wash. Poor John! People would tell him to enjoy his sleep while he could because when the baby came he wasn't going to get much sleep at night. Ha! I already had him broken in for that!

When the big night finally came, I answered the phone and it was Patty. She said that she and her husband were leaving for the hospital. I told her we were already half out the door! It was strange that, about the same time Patty started getting contractions, I woke up and looked at the clock and thought, "*This is it!*" Sure enough, a little while later we got the phone call from Patty.

To watch my son be born was the most wonderful thing in the world. They were great at the hospital. They asked if I wanted to clamp the cord and, naturally, I did. When they handed the baby to me, I was in heaven. I started to talk to my son and he just looked right at my face. My husband tells me that I would not shut up! I was even telling the baby about the two puppies at home waiting for him. My son's first sentence will probably be, "Mom, you talk too much!"

It takes a very special person to be a surrogate mother, and Patty was our special and loving person. There is a bond between Patty and me that will be there forever. Patty gave me the greatest thing in my life—she gave me my son!

If we decided to have another child, I would ask Patty and no one else. I was terrified to meet her at first, but now I would encourage everyone to do exactly what we did. I feel that the women involved should meet, share the pregnancy and make that bond—it's a good feeling.

Besides being thankful to Patty, we're also thankful to her husband for being the wonderful person he is, and to Patty's family for standing by her, as well as understanding exactly what she did for us and why . . .

Introduction

One out of every six couples in the United States who want children cannot have them because of infertility. Some couples turn to medical treatments or corrective surgery, others try to adopt, an avenue that is becoming increasingly difficult, as more and more unwed mothers either decide to keep their babies or to have abortions.

Of all the means employed by childless couples, Surrogate Mothering is really a method of last resort. Surrogate Mothering is simply another means of adoption, but biologically the baby belongs to the father, who, along with his wife, then adopts the baby.

A woman is artificially inseminated with the sperm of the father and carries the baby nine months. Then, she relinquishes her parental rights and the father and his wife adopt the child.

Some people believe Surrogate Mothering can be frustrating and expensive. Also, the process raises a host of legal and ethical questions. Surrogate Mothering is illegal in fourteen states. The program now exists in Kentucky, Michigan, Pennsylvania and California.

Under the Surrogate Mothering program, Surrogates set their own fees. In most cases the fees range from $7,500 to $12,000, with an average of $10,000.

The couple pays the Surrogate her fee in advance, but it is placed in escrow until the baby is born and blood tests have established the father's paternity.

The process is complete when the father and his wife legally adopt the baby.

The lawyers charge the couple varying rates for legal, medical, and psychological services. In most cases, the fee amounts to about $8,000, but the maximum is not higher than $10,000.

The program's toughest job is to ensure that the Surrogate will relinquish the baby to the couple and will not suffer any psychological damage from the experience.

One doctor believes that, under current Pennsylvania laws, a custody battle between the father and the Surrogate would result if the Surrogate decided to keep the baby. He states, "We think the couple would win the custody battle in the end."

To avoid legal problems, the program in Philadelphia, Pennsylvania, carefully screens the Surrogate and interviews the applicant to make sure she fully understands and accepts her role in this type of program. The most important factor is that she must think of herself only as a "carrier". She must divorce herself from any emotional ties to the baby. If she clears that initial hurdle, the applicant goes to the medical doctor and then to the psychologist for psychological testing and an in-depth interview.

The psychologist probes deeply into the Surrogate's inner self by examining her motivations, asking about her family life, and delving into any doubts or fears that she may mention.

He rules out women who have psychological problems, such as depression, that might make the experience difficult for them, as well as women he thinks might have trouble giving up the baby after the birth. He is also very cautious about accepting women who want to experience pregnancy for the very first time.

The best candidates are those women who have sympathy for the couple, or who decide to become Surrogate mothers because of their own financial needs. Many good Surrogates are women that are divorced and want the money to provide for their own children.

Once a Surrogate is accepted into the program, a profile is put together by the lawyers for the couple to examine. This information includes a color photograph of the Surrogate and any of her children, a medical history, a psychological description including details about her family background, the Surrogate's application, which gives her reasons for applying, as well as facts about her education, ethnic heritage, religion, hobbies and other personal details.

The program I was in did not try to match the couple and the Surrogate. They felt the couple could best decide what they wanted the mother of their child to be like. Other programs prefer to match the infertile couple to a specific Surrogate.

Personally, I think it is best for the couple to choose their Surrogate. That way, the couple has a say in who their Surrogate will be. They have the opportunity to find out about all the Surrogates in the program and are able to make the final decision as to which woman will carry their child.

Statistics say ninety percent of women who become pregnant from artificial insemination are pregnant after six attempts, while fifty percent are pregnant after three attempts.

Artificial insemination can be a painstaking process. Stress and anxiety can alter your menstrual cycle and hamper pregnancy, which leads to frustration and disappointment.

I was a Surrogate Mother for John and Sharon, an infertile couple. It was one of the best things I ever did in my life, even though I know how controversial the subject of Surrogate mothering can be.

It has been almost a year since I last gave birth. This birth was different from when I gave birth to my own two sons. During this particular birth, I delivered another son, but this time he was John and Sharon's son.

I would like to tell my story which, because of the circumstances, I feel is very unique. I also hope it will help people to understand more about the Surrogate Mothering Program.

Surrogate Mothering has many good points that adoption does not. I do believe Surrogate

Mothering is not for every individual, however.

I also believe that in years to come, Surrogate Mothering will be highly accepted by all, and will be simply another means of adoption.

There are three specific reasons that helped me to realize that part of my role in this life was to be a Surrogate Mother, particularly for John and Sharon. They are:

1. John and Sharon originally contacted a program in California, that in turn told them there was a program in Philadelphia.

2. When I first thought about being a Surrogate Mother, I contacted the program in Kentucky and became involved until I was pregnant with my own child. After the birth of my child, I was told about the program in Philadelphia.

3. The father and I meeting by coincidence when, in fact, the lawyers are against the meeting of the parties involved. This all led to John and Sharon witnessing the birth of their child.

After you read my story, you may be able to better comprehend why I so strongly feel that, even though this child is half mine biologically, I believe that he is very much John and Sharon's child, and they can truly call him their very own.

1

My Decision

I decided I wanted to be a Surrogate Mother about four years ago. The thought first came into my head when my husband and I were watching the ten o'clock news. There was a story on the news about a woman who had just given birth to a baby for an infertile couple. The couple had been trying for years to conceive their own child. The baby would be adopted by the couple when, in fact, the baby would already belong biologically to the man who was about to adopt the baby. I was really interested in the story. The more I thought about it, the more I felt that being a Surrogate Mother would be something I would really like to do for someone.

In the middle of the story, my husband started talking to me but I was so impressed by the Surrogate Mother's story that I said, "Honey, come here and listen to this!"

He came closer and we both sat there and listened to the rest of the story. Both of us were so impressed and touched by what this woman had done, that we started talking about the idea of Surrogate Mothering. The more we discussed it, the more I felt sure I wanted to do this, so I asked John, "How would you feel if I were to be a Surrogate Mother? Would it bother you that I was carrying another man's baby?"

At first, he just looked at me, and I could tell he was doing some heavy thinking. He finally said he thought it would really be nice if I could do it. Just think how the couple would feel once they saw the baby! It would be something you could give them that no one else could. He also said that if I decided to be a Surrogate, he would stand by me 100%.

That night, we talked about it at great length and also discussed the possibilities of negative reactions from some people, as well as the reactions of our friends and family.

But finally, we both agreed that no matter what kind of reactions we got from *anyone*, being a Surrogate Mother would well be worth it. To me, nothing anyone could do or say could change the fact of how much happiness a baby could add to a couple's life, particularly a couple that is not able to have a baby themselves, and who have been wanting one for years.

One factor that also helped in my decision was that when my husband and I decided to start our family, two years passed before we could conceive our first child. And in those two years, thoughts were always going through my head like, God, what if I can't have children! I always wanted them and always just assumed I'd have them. But every month then, nothing was happening, and thoughts about not having children was always on my mind. I had even gone to infertility doctors and had an operation to see why I wasn't getting pregnant. This is why I can really understand what infertile couples are going through, because I was almost there. Another factor is that I have good pregnancies. I enjoy being pregnant and I like how I feel during those nine months. My husband enjoys me when I'm pregnant and best of all, my labor and deliveries are short and easy.

I feel blessed that I can have children of my own. Since we are all children of God, I just felt God would be giving a couple a child through me.

I also realize what it means to me to be a mother and to raise a family. I can't imagine going through life without feeling the joy I get from my children, so I wanted to help another woman experience that, even if it meant carrying the child full-term and then giving it up after the birth. I truly feel fortunate that I can help someone in that way.

I'm sure if you have children, you can understand how great they are and all the joy they bring into your life.

The adoption process can be quite lengthy and there are some people who just don't want to wait, especially since many couples today do not decide to start having children until they are in their thirties. And now I hear that adoption agencies don't accept couples if they are past the age of 35. Also if a husband gets transferred quite often in his job, forget it. Adoption agencies consider such a home life unstable; therefore, a couple is not eligible for a child. So Surrogate Mothering does have a lot of advantages, the most important one being that you are inseminated with the husband's sperm. When the baby is born, biologically he is the husband's baby right from the start. Also, there isn't a seven year waiting list like most adoption agencies have. I think too, that if a couple is going to adopt a baby, they would rather adopt a baby who is biologically the father's than adopt a baby who doesn't belong to the father at all. And, with the Surrogate baby, the couple knows the biological mother's background, where with adoption, they know nothing about the mother or father.

The very next morning, I tried to contact the television station that showed the story the night before. After three separate attempts, I finally reached the right party. They gave me the name of the doctor who, at that time, was in Kentucky. I phoned him, and was told that I had to contact the lawyer's office, which I did.

I told the lawyer that I was very interested in their program, and wanted more information. We asked questions of each other, then the lawyer said they would send an application for me to fill out and return to them.

Within two weeks I received the application, filled it out and mailed it back to the lawyers. They were going to review it and get back in touch with me, either by mail or by telephone. Patiently, I awaited their reply.

I got a phone call from the lawyer in which he explained everything in detail, and told me that all I had to do now was wait for a couple to choose me for their Surrogate Mother. This took some time and, to my surprise, while waiting for their call, I found out I was pregnant with my second child!

The day after I found this out, I got the call from the lawyer, saying they had a couple who was interested in having me as their Surrogate. I explained that I was pregnant with my own child. They said they would place my file on inactive status until after the birth of my baby. I was real happy about being pregnant with our second child, but I did feel sad that I had to wait another year before I could become a Surrogate Mother.

In the next few months, I talked to my doctor about becoming a Surrogate Mother after the birth of our baby. I asked her if she would keep me as a patient and deliver the baby. She said that she would love to, but there was no reason why I had to go to Kentucky to get into the program, because there was a program right here in Philadelphia. She gave me the name of the doctor involved in the program, so I could keep it in a safe place until after I delivered and was ready once again to enter the Surrogate Mothering Program. I was really excited—now I wouldn't have to travel out of state.

Now I had just a few more months to wait. Then, finally, I would be able to enter the program and become a Surrogate Mother!

The next few months gave me time to think about what I was going to tell my friends, parents, and relatives. This was a big decision in my life, and I knew not everyone would understand why I was doing it. There would be a lot of positive and negative reactions, but I also knew that I could handle whatever happened. This was one thing in my life I was sure I wanted to do. The final decision of what to tell everyone was really the only one there was—to tell them "the truth". No matter how they felt, I would just have to accept their reactions. After thinking about being a Surrogate Mother for this long, I knew that no matter how much negativity I received on the subject, I would be able to keep a positive attitude. To me, this was the most important thing for the baby. I did hope, however, that my family and friends would understand that I wanted to do something really special for two other people and would applaud my decision and give me positive reactions and support. I would just have to wait and see!

2

Delay

The labor and delivery of my own child went well. In fact, when I had to go for my state boards to become a cosmetologist, I was four days past my due date. It was an all-day testing—a 1½ hour drive from our home. My mom kept begging me not to go, just in case I went into labor. I couldn't even think of this, because if I didn't go, they would reschedule me for my state boards the following month. If that happened, I would have a little baby to think about. What would I do with him all day? I was going to be nursing him, so I couldn't leave him for the whole day, but I definitely couldn't take him with me. So, I had no other choice but to go and take my state boards that day. I knew I was really taking a chance of going into labor—after all, I was four days late, but I would have plenty of time to get to the hospital.

I got up early that morning and was feeling good. I was starting to get little contractions, but couldn't tell anyone or they would insist that I stay home. I went over to pick up my cousin, Cindy, who was going to be my model during the testing. When I arrived at her house, she just looked at me and shook her head. She couldn't believe I was actually going to take my boards!

We arrived there in plenty of time. As the testing started, some judges even commented that I looked like I was due any minute. When I told them I was due four days ago, they looked at me like I was crazy. Due to the fact that I could go into labor any minute, I thought maybe they would hurry me along with all the tests, but they didn't. Within six hours, the testing was finally over and we were on our way home. We stopped to get some lunch, and by then the contractions were coming more frequently. They still weren't very strong, but I really felt that I would be delivering the baby within the next day or two.

We arrived home about 4 p.m.; everyone being very glad to see us. I must have had ten phone calls from relatives and friends to make sure I was home and hadn't delivered the baby somewhere on the turnpike!

My husband and I went out to dinner that night, then came home to watch television and make popcorn. John Matthew was in bed. I was sitting on the living room floor, timing the contractions to see how close they were coming.

It was 10 p.m. when I looked at my husband and said, "Honey, I think we're going to the hospital tonight". Only seconds later, my contractions started getting stronger and then, my water broke!

Should I call the doctor? I wondered. My contractions were only ten minutes apart. I started getting my things ready for the hospital. In a matter of minutes, the contractions became *very* strong and were five minutes apart. I decided it was time to call my doctor. She said she would meet us at the hospital and to take our time driving; she was aware we had to take John Matthew to my mother-in-law's house.

I woke John up and my husband carried him out to the car. I brought my bag out. We had a half-hour drive, then another 20 minutes to the hospital. When we came to the bridge that went over to Philadelphia, John asked me how I was doing.

I replied, "I think they're now two minutes apart. Please try not to go over any bumps!" The contractions weren't bad, but the bumps, forget it!

When we finally reached my mother-in-law's, John Matthew didn't want me to leave. He kept saying, "Don't leave me, Mommy, I want you to stay here with me."

Like any mother, there I was sitting on the bed, rocking him in my arms and trying to comfort him. Meanwhile, my husband was standing at the door, saying, "Patty, if we don't leave now, we'll never make it to the hospital." As hard as it was to leave John Matthew, I knew we had to leave right away, or I would have the baby right there!

We reached the hospital at 1 a.m. Everything went smoothly. In fact, we had my brother's sound movie camera to record the birth. I think the nurses thought we were both crazy! Here I was in hard labor, telling my husband to hurry and get the camera ready, so we wouldn't miss the birth. My husband was trying to get the camera ready as well as helping me with the breathing during the contractions!

Everything was ready—I was about to deliver, John finally had the camera focused, and

Ann, the midwife, was ready for the birth. I started to push. Everything seemed to be going fine until I heard Ann tell the nurse to go get a doctor. From the look on Ann's face, John could tell something was wrong. He put the camera down and walked over to her to see what the problem was. Ann said the baby's shoulders were turned and weren't coming the way they should.

"I have to push," I told her.

"Okay," she said.

Within minutes, the baby's head was out and everything was fine! That's right—John missed the head popping out, but got the rest of the birth on film! I was a little disappointed that he missed it, but then, he was only concerned about us and wanted to make sure we weren't in any danger. So, at 3:11 a.m., Michael was born—8 lbs., 11 oz.

We spent about an hour alone with Michael before he had to go to the nursery. We called our parents to tell them they had a new grandson.

All I could think about at that moment was taking a shower. A nurse let me use the shower in the nurse's station, so I kissed John and said I'd be back in a few minutes. John decided to call his mom back to tell her to put a pot of coffee on; he was too excited to go home and sleep. Instead, he wanted to tell everyone about the birth of his son!

I, on the other hand, was now standing in the shower thinking how lucky I was to have two precious sons, a wonderful husband, and by the grace of God to be able to carry and deliver children so easily. My second thought was that now I could call the lawyers and tell them I was ready to be a Surrogate Mother. I could now give birth again, but this time, it would be for another couple. *They* could have the same wonderful experience that John and I just had!

3

The Program

About three weeks later, I contacted the doctor who was in the Surrogate Mothering program here in the area. I spoke with his nurse, and told her I was interested in being a Surrogate Mother. She gave me the number of the lawyers and said I would have to contact them. I did so, and made an appointment to find out more about the Philadelphia program.

At this point, I started wondering when and what to actually tell people. Both my husband and I had tried to decide what was best to tell everyone, once I became pregnant. But we hadn't come up with any definite answers yet, except the truth.

We thought about telling only the family and letting everyone else think that the baby was really ours, since we had already decided to leave the area after the baby's birth. A year before, my husband and I had purchased land in Virginia. We planned to build a home which we had designed five years ago. We never had the opportunity to build until we made this purchase, so we were looking forward to the move.

As things happened, my husband started to build our home at the same time I started the inseminations. This worked out perfectly. John lived in a trailer on the land during the eight months he worked on the house, while I stayed in New Jersey with the boys. I had to be available for the inseminations each month. I saw my husband about every two weeks, unless it was time for the inseminations, at which time I'd miss going to Virginia. There was no way I wanted to have the slight nagging thought that the baby was fathered by my husband!

I remember the episode with the Surrogate Mother in Michigan, who gave birth. The baby was actually her husband's. I wanted to be 100% sure the baby I carried belonged to the infertile couple. That is one reason it wasn't hard for me to have my husband so far away those eight months. In fact, it made things a lot easier. I knew us being separated would all be worth it—I'd know for sure the baby wasn't ours, and we would get the house we always dreamed about.

After tossing around different things to tell everyone, the only one I could be comfortable with was the truth, that I was a Surrogate Mother. I still had plenty of time to think about this, however—I wasn't even in the program yet. I still had an appointment to talk with the lawyers to find out how the program worked. Besides, I was still nursing Michael, so it would still be some time before I could actually start the inseminations.

I was very excited about talking with the lawyers. When I walked into their building, I wondered if anyone would know why I was there. I went into the office and gave my name to the secretary.

I only waited ten minutes. The lawyer explained the program in detail. She then gave me an application to fill out in her office. I had to include my name, address, education, color of hair and eyes, and hobbies. There were also questions about my background and family. It was somewhat like an employment application. Then there was one question which pretty much stunned me—what fee did I want? I hadn't given it much thought. In fact, I didn't even know money was involved. Of course, I knew the couple paid for all medical expenses and any bills pertaining to the pregnancy, but a fee, too? I had to think about that question. I also had to talk with my husband. The lawyer said I could take the application home and talk about the fee with my husband, then return the application within a few days.

Then I asked her, "What do the other Surrogates put down for the fee?" I had no idea, and I was sure John would ask me what the other Surrogates received. She said it was entirely up to the individual, but most Surrogates got anywhere from $7,500 to $13,000.

She also explained that before I could get into the program, I had to go to their medical doctor for an examination. I also had to go to their psychologist to see if he thought I was a good candidate for the program. Then, if I was approved, they would put my file in their inactive files until after I had finished nursing Michael. She gave me the names of the doctors and thanked me for coming in. She said that I would hear from her after I saw the doctors, and after she received both doctors' reports.

As I walked out, I thought, "Well, I've finally started the process of becoming a Surrogate Mother."

As soon as I arrived home, I made both phone calls to set up my appointments, one in March with the medical doctor and the other in April with the psychologist. I can't tell you how happy I felt at that point!

February went fast, and now I was on my way to Elkins Park to see the doctor. It took me about 45 minutes to get there. When I walked in, the office was more crowded than I had expected. I gave my name to the receptionist and sat down. I looked around, wondering if any of these girls were going to be Surrogates also. I wanted to talk to them to find out but thought it might be better to read a magazine instead, until it was my turn to see the doctor.

As it turned out, the appointment was just a regular routine visit with an examination. The doctor asked me a few questions. He told me I was in excellent health. After I was accepted into the program, I was to call him as soon as I got my period, so I could make another appointment to begin the inseminations.

Now *that* part was finished, and I was looking forward to seeing the psychologist. I didn't have any idea how that appointment would go but I only had a few weeks before I'd find out. I rode home, wondering if everything would work out as I hoped.

4

Family and Friends

In March, I decided to tell my family and some of my close friends what I was about to do. I thought it would be better to tell them before I became pregnant than wait until after I was pregnant, and started showing.

First, I wanted to tell my parents. Well, that didn't go over as well as I would have liked. One day, they came over to our house. As we were sitting around talking, I wondered how I was going to start the conversation.

Before I knew it, I just blurted out the news. "Guess what I'm going to do? Become a Surrogate Mother!" I didn't even give them a chance to answer.

My dad didn't say a word. I think he went into shock! All my mom said was, "Please don't!"

Then I said this was something that I had given much thought to—and really wanted to help another woman have a child. I thought they would start asking me questions, but instead, they just got up and walked out of the house. Now I was the one who went into shock this time!

I looked at my husband and said, "What happened?"

He wasn't quite sure either, so for the time being, I left the situation like that. I waited for my parents to bring up the subject again but, even after several months, they never said anything about it. I had to bring the subject up again myself, but each time I did, they either changed the subject, or told me they just didn't want to talk about it. I had hoped they would ask me some questions. I felt I had to at least get something solved before I actually did get pregnant. What was I going to do —wait until I had a big belly, then talk about it? I didn't want that to happen.

Well, who was next after my parents? I decided to try my grandmother and Aunt

Audrey. I'd been close to both of them over the last few years and was always over to their house. The house is my aunt's and my gram has her own apartment in the back of the house. As I was driving over, I tried to think of a different approach to use in telling them about what I planned to do.

I walked in and they were both there, sitting at my aunt's kitchen table. I sat down very casually and my Aunt Audrey got me a glass of iced tea. I was still wondering about how to start the conversation. After we talked awhile, I decided to ask them if they had ever heard of Surrogate Mothering.

"Why?" they both asked.

I replied, "Well, I was thinking of being a Surrogate Mother and wanted to know how you both would feel."

This time I got some response. They asked a lot of questions and I told them all about the program and my reasons for wanting to be in it.

At first my gram was looking at me a little strangely. Then after I had explained the program she said, "My God, Patty, at first I thought you and that guy would have to . . ."

"No, Gram," I said, "they use artificial insemination."

"Thank goodness!" she exclaimed. Then she said she thought it was a nice thing for me to do.

My Aunt Audrey thought it was really nice for the couple—but she didn't think she could do it. She asked, "What if it's a girl?" Then she said she'd feel bad for my parents if it were, because my mom was always hoping for a granddaughter.

When I was pregnant with Michael, my two brothers' wives were also pregnant. We were all due around the same time and my mom thought that between the three of us she'd at least get one granddaughter. But—to her surprise—she got three beautiful grandsons!

So that was my aunt's only concern about my wanting to enter the Surrogate Mothering program. After we all talked some more, I was very glad that I had decided to tell them—if only my parents could have been that easy.

We decided that the next relatives to break the news to would be my mother-in-law, Pearl, and my sister-in-law, Dulcie. We go to their house every Saturday night but this night was going to be different as we were going to tell them what I was about to do.

As we sat around the kitchen table, my husband, John, just came right out with it, "Mom, what would you think if Patty were to be a Surrogate Mother?"

She took a few seconds to answer but finally said, "If it's something you both want, then it's O.K. with me."

After I had the baby, Pearl told me that a lot of remarks had been made by people she worked with which really hurt her. Most of the time Pearl would just reply, "You have to be someone special to give a life."

My sister-in-law, Dulcie, thought at first that we were doing it for the money but by the end of the night, after much talking, she realized that it was much more than that.

Now it was time to tell my two brothers and their wives. One brother thought it was immoral, so I didn't bother to discuss it with his wife. She, in turn, never discussed it with me until later on. My other brother and his wife thought it was great, because they knew couples who were having trouble getting pregnant and understood how they felt. Out of everyone I told, they accepted the news the best—until after I actually gave birth to the baby.

The neighbors took it well, too. One couple was very supportive throughout the pregnancy. They lived in the apartment in front of us. Michelle babysat our two sons while I worked. I saw Michelle every day and felt very comfortable around her. She always talked to me about the baby and the couple. She was great!

My close friends—well, they really didn't talk a whole lot about it. They just wanted to know if I would be okay during the pregnancy, and prayed I wouldn't have any regrets after the baby was born. Not until after the birth did I realize how concerned they really were. It made me feel good to know they cared that much about me.

Also, at the time, I was working full time with three girls. Naturally, I had to tell them too. They were neither for it nor against it. They just wanted to know how I could do it as they didn't think they could.

I felt better that I told some people, regardless if they accepted it or not. When I became pregnant and started to show, I would have no explaining to do.

5

Getting Chosen

It was finally time for my appointment with the psychologist. We were having friends from Kentucky, who were in the area on vacation, over for dinner. While my husband entertained them, I ran over for my 7 p.m. appointment.

I was somewhat nervous about going, and, I have to admit, I was very curious and excited. What was it going to be like? What would he ask me? What will we talk about? When I

finally walked into the office, there was absolutely no one around, no receptionist or
patients. Was I in the wrong building? I didn't
think so, so I just sat down and waited. I
really felt a little strange, but then I heard
voices and the door opened. The doctor
popped his head out the door and said he'd be
with me in a minute.

Within ten minutes, a man walked out, followed by the doctor, who introduced himself
and shook my hand as I told him who I was.
We sat down in his office. I guess I looked
somewhat nervous because he asked me if I
felt comfortable. I said yes, but had to admit
I was a little nervous, since I had never been
to a psychologist before. I had no idea what
we were going to talk about. He assured me
that the questions he was about to ask were
very general and there was no reason for me
to be nervous.

He was right. As we started talking, I felt
more at ease with him and enjoyed our visit. I
told him about myself when I was growing up
—about my family and, best of all, my husband and sons. He also asked me about my
life in general; school, relatives, friends. He
went on to ask about my marriage and how I
felt as a wife and mother. I think he covered
everything—from the time I was born to that
very moment I was sitting in his office.

I felt good about myself when I left his office, after being there for an hour and a half. He told me that I had a good outlook on life. In his opinion, I would make an excellent Surrogate Mother. I was pleased to hear him say that, because that was exactly how I felt. It takes a certain kind of person to be a Surrogate. I felt lucky to have those qualities.

As I was riding home, I thought about my childhood. I realized that I would do some things differently, now that I am a mother. When I was growing up, I had two brothers, one older than me, one younger. We aren't a real close family now, not like I wish we were.

In high school, two of my closest friends had mothers who also seemed to be their best friends. I always wanted a relationship like that when I had children! When I was growing up, my mom was just my mom. I didn't feel like we were close friends—just mother and daughter. She wasn't someone I could go to when I had a problem or questions. After all, she was just my *mom*!

As it turned out, now, my mother and I have become best friends. It took a lot of growing up on my part. As I started having my own children, I realized how important it really is to have a close relationship with your parents. I left home to live on my own when I was eighteen years old, and was always too busy to go visit my parents.

Now that I'm married and have my own

family, I realize that I wasn't the daughter I should have been. I suppose that's how it is with most teenagers. I just wish I would have realized when I was younger how important the relationship should be between parents and their children. Now that I have children of my own, I try to be their friend as well as their mother. I hope as they get older we'll always remain a close family.

As far as my marriage and how I feel about that? I think I am very lucky to have the husband I have. To us, our marriage is something special. What does my husband think about me being a Surrogate Mother? He has no problem at all with the idea of me carrying another man's baby. In fact, he enjoys it when I am pregnant. He gave me so much support throughout my pregnancies—he was terrific!

Now that both my appointments were over, I had to wait to hear if I would be accepted into the program. Within a few weeks, I received a letter saying that I was approved, but my application would be put in the inactive file until I was finished nursing Michael. They did tell me that I could go ahead and send them a picture of myself, along with a picture of both my sons. These were to go in my file so when the time came, the adoptive couple could see what we all looked like.

I was really excited to have been accepted into the program; now I had to get those pictures together. Did you ever go through your family pictures and not find one decent picture of yourself? I searched and searched, but none were good enough. This picture had to be special. After all, it was going to be sent to the couple. I felt that the picture would be a factor as to whether or not they would want me for their Surrogate Mother.

So off to the store for film I went. My husband clicked away until we had a good picture. We finally selected a picture of me and my oldest son standing in the back yard and another picture of our youngest son sitting in his crib. At the time, Michael was only a few months old. But it was such a cute picture of him, I thought it would be all right to send two separate pictures, rather than one with all of us in it. The next day I enclosed the pictures in an envelope and sent them on their way to the lawyer's office.

As the months went by, my feelings were really becoming torn—not about being a Surrogate, but about nursing Michael. I loved nursing my children and I believed it was the best thing for them. Yet I was anxious for Michael to stop. Once he stopped, I could go ahead and start the inseminations. I knew I could have weaned him myself, but wouldn't feel really comfortable if I did. So, I patiently waited until Michael was ready to stop nursing by himself.

John Matthew had nursed until a week before his second birthday! I knew Michael was going to be different; Michael didn't nurse as much as John, so I had the feeling he would stop a lot earlier. I was right; by the time Michael was nine months old, he completely weaned himself.

I called the lawyers to tell them they could start sending out my composite to the different couples. In turn, they told me that as soon as I was chosen, they'd let me know.

I don't remember exactly how long it took, but it seemed like within weeks I got the call I had been waiting for. It was the lawyer! He told me I had been chosen by an infertile couple and they wanted me to carry their baby. Boy, I can't begin to tell you how happy I was! I remember thinking how happy and excited the couple must feel to have finally found the woman who would be their baby's Surrogate Mother. Within a year or so, they would finally have a baby of their own!

The lawyer told me he would get the contract drawn up and get back to us. Then we would make an appointment with him to go over the contract, so we understood everything we were about to do.

The next few weeks, my husband and I talked about what we thought would be in the contract, and what things we wanted to put in it, if they weren't already in there. One item my husband and I both wanted in the contract was that, once I gave birth, the couple could not change their minds about taking the child. I'm sure they wanted the same thing, but the other way around—that I wouldn't change *my* mind after giving birth and decide to keep the baby.

It took only a week for the lawyers to get the contract ready. As we sat in the lawyer's office going over the contract, the lawyer advised us to take it home, read it thoroughly, and get our own lawyer to go over it with us, just to make sure we knew and understood everything. So we did just that, and decided to delete some things and to add others.

I wanted one clause taken out of the contract completely. It had to do with me having an abortion if something was wrong with the baby. There was no way I was going to get an abortion—under *any* circumstance! Besides, there was another clause stating that the couple would assume all legal responsibilities for any child born to Surrogate, regardless of any birth defects, congenital abnormalities or any other medical problems. To me, that clause took care of the whole matter.

One item I wanted added was that the wife would still adopt the baby if anything happened to her husband prior to the birth of the baby. I also wanted an insurance policy taken out in the event both the father and his wife passed away prior to the birth, with me having the right to keep the child and also being the beneficiary of said insurance policy. I also wanted an insurance policy taken out on myself in case something happened to me during the pregnancy or delivery. All the changes were made and presented to the couple. They accepted the changes and the contract was signed by all parties.

I need to tell you this, because it upset me very much. Also, it may help other Surrogate Mothers with their contracts. In my seventh month of pregnancy I found out that the lawyers never took out the insurance policy on me, naming my husband as the beneficiary. The insurance policy was supposed to state that, in the event I passed away, my husband would receive $50,000 to take care of our own children. Well, when I finally got the application to fill out, I called the insurance company. When they found out I was already seven months pregnant, they said it was too late to take out the policy. You can imagine how upset I was! I called the lawyer to ask why they waited so long to send the application. He said there was a mix-up, but not to worry about it.

"Don't worry about it? The insurance company is not going to let me take out the policy now, so what are you going to do?"

"Patty, don't worry. Nothing is going to happen to you. You're healthy, and besides, you have already given birth to your own two children, so what could possibly happen?"

I told him that wasn't the point—they were supposed to take out the policy and didn't do it!

I then asked him, "God forbid, if I *did* die, who would pay my husband the money that was supposed to come from the policy?"

He said that he would have to take it out of his own pocket, since it was in the contract!

I really didn't think he would. At this point I was very upset, but there was nothing I could do. I tried to forget about it so the baby wouldn't feel how upset I was. It was really important to me to stay as calm and happy throughout this pregnancy, so the baby would feel that way too.

6

The Contract

The contract was very thorough. It was about 16 pages long and covered just about everything possible to protect both the infertile couple and the Surrogate Mother. Here is an outline of the contract to give you some idea of what it contained:

1. The contract is between the Surrogate and her husband and the Natural father and his wife.

2. It states that the Natural father is married and desires to have his bodily sperm implanted by artificial insemination in a woman who shall carry said child through to term (hereinafter referred to as "Surrogate") bearing a child biologically related to Natural father.

3. Surrogate desires to have the sperm of Natural father artificially inseminated in her body for the purpose of carrying Natural father's child through to delivery, when the Natural father and his wife will adopt any and all children born to the Surrogate.

4. Surrogate and her husband will not form or attempt to form a parent-child relationship with any child she may conceive and shall freely, voluntarily, and readily terminate all parental rights to each child.

5. Surrogate and husband agree not to see the child after the birth nor to interfere in any way with any rights of the Natural father and his wife.

6. Natural father will pay all medical, hospitalization, pharmaceutical, laboratory and therapy expenses incurred in the Surrogate's pregnancy not covered or allowed by insurance.

7. Natural father shall not be responsible for lost wages of Surrogate or her husband, child care expenses, clothing, or any expenses

for emotional/mental conditions/problems related to said pregnancy.

8. Surrogate agrees to abide by Physician's instructions to monitor and regulate her menstrual cycle and further agrees to be present for all insemination procedures as directed by the Physician.

9. Natural father shall pay, immediately after Surrogate becomes pregnant, for the cost of a one year term life insurance policy on the life of Surrogate with the Surrogate having the right to designate the beneficiary thereunder.

10. Immediately after the birth of the child, Surrogate, Natural father, and child shall undergo such medical tests as required by Physician, including HLA testing. In the event that it is determined by Physician that child is not biologically related to Natural father, said determination shall constitute a breach of this agreement on the part of the Surrogate and the Natural father shall have no obligations or liability under this contract. Further, Surrogate shall reimburse Natural father for all expenses incurred in connection with this contract.

11. Surrogate and her husband fully and completely understand and agree to assume any and all risks, including the possible risk of death, which are incident to artificial con-

ception, pregnancy, childbirth and postpartum complications.

12. In the event that child is miscarried prior to the fifteenth week of pregnancy, no compensation shall be paid to the Surrogate, however, any expenses shall be paid or reimbursed to Surrogate. In the event that child is miscarried between the fifteenth and the thirty-second week of pregnancy, Surrogate shall receive twenty-five percent of the compensation in addition to any expenses. In the event of a miscarriage or stillbirth after the thirty-second week of pregnancy, Surrogate shall be entitled to receive fifty percent of the compensation in addition to any expenses.

13. Surrogate and Natural father shall undergo a complete physical and genetic evaluation, under the direction and supervision of the Physician designated by Surrogate Mother to determine whether the physical health and well being of each is satisfactory. Said physical examination shall include whatever testing and/or examination is deemed appropriate by said Physician, including any testing for venereal disease.

14. Surrogate's husband agrees to periodic testing and/or examination for venereal diseases at the request of physician retained as a consultant by the lawyers.

15. Natural father agrees that he will not seek to learn the identity of Surrogate and/or

husband, or their family, and will not advise child of said identity if it shall become known.

16. Surrogate and her husband warrant and represent that they shall not seek to learn the identity of Natural father of child or his wife and will not attempt to contact child if Natural father's identity becomes known.

17. Provided Surrogate is not in breach of this contract, and in the event Surrogate's pregnancy has not occurred within a period of six menstrual cycles, this contract shall terminate by written notice from the attorney for Natural father to Surrogate and/or her husband.

18. Surrogate and/or her husband agree that they will provide no public media interviews relating to this matter whereby Surrogate and/or Natural father may be identified, without the written consent of Natural father and/or the lawyers.

19. The parties agree that the child shall be delivered by an obstetrician selected by the Surrogate subject to approval of lawyers and the doctor who did the inseminations.

20. Surrogate agrees to adhere to all medical instructions given to her by Physician. Surrogate also agrees not to smoke cigarettes, drink any alcoholic beverages, use any illegal drugs, non-prescription medications, or prescribed medications, without the written consent from Physician. Surrogate also

agrees not to participate in dangerous sports or activities, be exposed to radiation, toxic chemicals or to be exposed to communicable illnesses.

21. Surrogate and/or her husband will meet with the professional psychologist retained by lawyers on such occasions as required by said Physician.

22. Surrogate agrees to follow a pre-natal medical examination schedule as specified by Physicians.

23. Surrogate shall adhere to a mandatory requirement to take all medicine and vitamins prescribed by her treating obstetrician and/or physician. Surrogate shall make sure that her activity level conforms to the recommendations of her treating obstetrician and physician and shall submit to an amniocentesis test and/or ultrasound survey at the request of her treating obstetrician or physician. Failure to conform to any of this will constitute a breach of contract by the Surrogate.

24. In the event Surrogate and/or her husband fail to terminate parental rights pursuant to the provisions of this contract, such action will constitute a breach of said contract and Surrogate and/or husband will forfeit their rights to any fees and be responsible for any medical costs and other expenses incurred. In addition, Surrogate and/or her

husband will immediately reimburse Natural father all monies which Natural father already paid.

25. Surrogate authorizes the release to Natural father all medical and psychological records relating to Surrogate. It is understood that said records shall have Surrogate's identity deleted therefrom.

26. Each party fully understands this agreement and they are signing voluntarily. They also agree that they sought the advice of a legal counsel who has explained their rights and obligations of this contract.

27. This contract will be executed in two or more counterparts, each of which shall be an original but, all of which shall constitute one and the same, in order to maintain the confidentiality of all parties involved.

28. In witness whereof, the parties have, on the following pages set their hands and seals in order to preserve the confidentiality of their respective identities.

7

Insemination

Within a few months after signing the contract, it was finally time to start the inseminations. I called the doctor to set up an appointment. Within a week I went to see him. He explained to me that I had to keep a temperature chart for a few months so he could determine when I would ovulate. Boy, was I disappointed! I thought we would start the inseminations right then. I wasn't aware it would be a few more months before we could start. I knew how I felt about waiting, now I wondered how the couple felt about waiting another few months. I guess it wouldn't seem that long to them. After all, they've waited so long after trying to conceive their own child.

I went home and bought a basal thermometer. The next morning I started taking my temperature and keeping a chart. After the first month, I took it over for the doctor to see. It wasn't a very good chart to go by, so he had me keep another chart the following month. Maybe *this* one would be good enough to start the inseminations. At the end of that month, I went back to the doctor's office. After we went over my chart, the doctor decided we could go ahead with the inseminations the following month. He determined that I ovulated between the fifteenth and the nineteenth day of my cycle. I was to call him after I got my period that month to set up an appointment to start the inseminations.

When I left his office, I was so happy! Riding home, all I could think about was how happy the couple was going to feel when the doctor called to tell them we were going to start trying to conceive their child the following month.

Well, that month when I got my period, I was so excited. It was a Sunday so I couldn't call the doctor until the following day. That night I started to get mixed emotions about everything. I was finally ready for the inseminations and was thrilled to death about it, but also scared about the whole idea. I was about to conceive a child with another man's sperm and carry the baby for nine months, then give up all my parental rights. I was real comfortable with that part of it. I guess my concerns now were trying to explain to everyone I was about to become a Surrogate Mother and listening to their comments. I also wondered deep down how my husband was going to handle the whole thing. He did tell me he supported me one hundred percent, but if a lot of people start asking you, "How can anyone's husband allow his wife to carry another man's baby?", it makes you wonder if they're right. Some were also constantly telling me this would hurt our relationship and marriage. These are thoughts I would rather not have in my consciousness, because I knew that what I was doing was absolutely right for me. I also know my husband better than anyone else and I knew for sure how he felt about me being a Surrogate Mother. My husband and I have a very "special" relationship and marriage. I knew how sincere he was in supporting me in wanting to do this. In fact, he gave me a lot of credit for wanting to carry a baby for another woman. Knowing that, I never had second thoughts about whether I should be doing this or not, but other people's comments did intrude on my peace of mind.

That weekend, I wondered just how everyone was going to react to me carrying another man's baby. I came to the conclusion really fast that it didn't matter at all to me what people thought. I was so sure I wanted to be a Surrogate Mother. Every time I thought about the fact that I was going to have a baby for a woman who really wanted a child more than anything, I just knew it was meant to be.

I don't want to go into great lengths on the subject of religion, but I do have to tell you that I believe in reincarnation. So not to go against what God would want me to do, I called and spoke with a nun about me becoming a Surrogate Mother. We spoke a few times in the course of a few weeks and after talking with her, I felt even better about my decision. The conclusion in our conversation was, "to go with the feelings I had in my heart." And believe me, I never felt as good about anything I did in my life, as my decision to be a Surrogate Mother.

On Monday I called the doctor to find out the dates he was going to inseminate me. I had to get inseminated two times a month, a day apart, either on the fifteenth and seventeenth day of my cycle or the sixteenth and eighteenth day. My appointment was made for the fifteenth day at 10:00 a.m.

I started to wonder how it was going to be done and whether or not I'd run into the natural father and his wife. I remember riding over to the office, while looking at each and every car I passed, wondering if it were the couple or not.

As I parked my car, I wondered if they were sitting in the parking lot watching me walk into the doctor's office. Perhaps we would be in the elevator together. I knew they knew exactly what I looked like, but I didn't know who they were or what they looked like—I wouldn't even know them if we were standing in the elevator together. Well, I didn't see a man that day, or even a couple, so I guess they got there in plenty of time to get into the office and out before I arrived for my appointment.

I finally got into the examination room. I sat on the table and waited for the doctor to come in. I saw a little container on the sink and wondered if that was the sperm. There was hardly anything in it.

I was too curious, so when the doctor walked in, I had to ask. "Is that the sperm?" When he said yes, I couldn't believe it! There were one, maybe two drops.

I guess the doctor knew what I was thinking because he said, "Patty, that's all it takes, what did you expect? A full cup?" Little did he know, that's *exactly* what I thought, but I was too embarrassed to say so.

He also explained to me that he scheduled the father to come in an hour earlier than me, so we wouldn't run into one another. He did the insemination and to my surprise, it only took a few seconds. He took an instrument that looked like a straw, put it in the container of sperm, got the sperm into the straw, then released the sperm into my cervix. I didn't feel a thing. Then I had to lie on the table for about twenty to thirty minutes to let the sperm penetrate into my uterus. That was it!

After the insemination, I still had to keep my temperature in the mornings to see if it dropped or stayed up. If it dropped, that meant I'd be getting my period and if my temperature stayed up, it meant I was pregnant. That month my temperature dropped. I wasn't that disappointed, after all, it was only the first attempt.

The inseminations started the beginning of March. By the end of the month, my husband was on his way to Virginia to start building our house. At times, there was pressure on me, especially with me being alone with the two boys. I had a lot of things going on in my life at that time. I was always wondering if and when the inseminations would take, whether or not my husband would run into any problems building the house, and just being separated from one another. Overall, I thought we handled everything pretty well.

I kept telling myself that once the house was done and we were all living down there, I'd look back and say, "It was all worth it!"

8

Meeting the Father

Each time I went to the doctor, I hoped to run into the couple. I really wanted to know what they looked like and a little about their life. By the third month of inseminations I hadn't seen the couple yet, so I decided to write to the mother. As I had no way of mailing the letter to her, I made an appointment with the lawyer to ask him if he would send it to her.

I wanted to write her because I felt very strongly about her and her husband being with me during labor and delivery. I wanted to tell her this, and see if they wanted to be there.

So I made an appointment and went over to the lawyer's office to give him the letter. I also wanted to ask him some questions about the couple. I just didn't think it was fair for the couple to know all about me and for me to know nothing about them. I asked the lawyer if he could please tell me a little bit about them. He did, but it wasn't as much as I had hoped. He told me they were both in their early thirties and they were the All-American type. They lived outside the city in a small town, and had a small family business. He also told me that the wife reminded him of me, that we looked similar, with about the same height and weight. If I ever met them, he was sure I would like them.

It was at that meeting that I explained to the lawyer how important it was for me to have the couple there at the birth. I told him that was what I said in the letter, and would he please mail it? He took the letter and said he would, and when he received an answer from the couple, he would mail it to me immediately. I asked him how he felt about them being in the birthing room with me. He replied, if that's what all of us wanted, he would agree, but he really would rather not have the couple know who their Surrogate was.

As I think back, I feel that if I had left it up to the lawyer to make sure the couple made it for the birth, he would not have done anything. I didn't really think he would make much of an effort to get the couple to the hospital on time to see the birth of their child. I'm glad now that I took matters into my own hands!

A few weeks later, I received two letters, one from the lawyer, along with one from the mother. Hers was such a sweet letter, I can't tell you how many times I read it, and every time I did, it brought tears to my eyes.

She explained both she and her husband would like very much to witness the birth of their baby. She also wanted to keep in touch with me during the pregnancy. I knew if we did, we would have to write through the lawyer, which I didn't like because I was sure the lawyer would read the letter first to make sure we didn't get too personal and find out things that we shouldn't.

Well, that was the first and last letter that went through the lawyers. The rest of them were mailed directly to each of our homes! There were no letters written through the inseminations. I think we were both waiting for something to happen so we would have something to write about.

When I received the letter from the couple saying they wanted to be with me in the birthing room, I went over to the lawyer to see if he could arrange for us to meet. I didn't want to meet the couple for the first time while I was in labor. I would have felt much more comfortable if we could meet before that!

The only reply he had for me was, "Well, let's wait and see what happens, we still have to get you pregnant first."

As soon as he said that, I had a feeling he wasn't going to let us meet, let alone try and get them to the hospital for the birth.

Just as I was thinking that he said, "Chances are—when you go into labor, it will be a Saturday afternoon. When I try to call the couple, they will be at a football game and I won't be able to get in touch with them."

Now I knew it! He really didn't want them there and he didn't want us to meet one another. Now, I was the only one who could make that happen and believe me, somehow, I would find a way! I wanted them with me more than anything in this whole pregnancy. I was already sure the mother wanted to be there along with her husband to see their baby born.

So each month that followed, I would pray I'd run into the couple at the doctor's office, so I could talk with them. But each time, I saw neither the father or his wife.

It was in the fourth month of the inseminations that I had to go on a Saturday morning. My appointment was at 9:00 a.m. and I was in a hurry because I had to go right to work afterwards. For some reason or another, I had to take the boys with me to the doctor, then drop them off at the babysitters on my way to work. I got to the doctor's office only five minutes early, but I sat in the car to make sure I didn't go into his office too early. Exactly at 9:00 a.m., I got out of the car and walked into the building. I had to get into the elevator and go to the second floor, with the boys right by my side. I don't remember seeing any other cars in the parking lot, so I felt sure the father wasn't still there. As we came out of the elevator and walked toward the doctor's door, I heard voices—*men's* voices, and they were coming from the doctor's office. Oh, no, what was I going to do? Could one of them be the father? I thought of running down the hall and hiding around the corner, but I was afraid he would open the door and see me running. I couldn't do that—besides, my two sons would probably think I was nuts! Instead, I just stood there—frozen.

Then the door knob turned. I thought, well, I just can't stand here when he walks out. I walked towards the door, and we both opened the door at the same time—and just stood there, looking at one another. I was too embarrassed to do anything, so we just said "Hi". He had his arm on the door, holding it open. I quickly walked into the office, my face as red as a tomato. He said goodbye to the doctor and left. In the examining room, I had to ask to make sure that was the father. The doctor said, "Who else?"

After the doctor did the insemination, I lay there for some twenty to thirty minutes, thinking. As embarrassed as I was, I was relieved to see what the father looked like. He had the appearance of being happily married and really wanting this child. This, of course, is what I had hoped for—to be a Surrogate Mother for a happily married couple who desperately wanted a baby.

The inseminations that month didn't take and we had to try again the following month. During that month, I was inseminated the two days as scheduled, but two days after the last insemination, my temperature was still up. I was a little confused, because it was now the nineteenth day of my cycle and I wondered if something was wrong. But the next morning my temperature dropped. That's right, I was ovulating! I called the doctor to tell him and also to ask him if he could call the couple to tell them. Maybe they would drive to the office to try another insemination.

The doctor said, "No, let's just wait till next month."

I was really upset with his answer and I let him know about it, "Hey, I'm real excited about getting pregnant for this couple and I'm sure they feel the same way. I have a feeling if you called them, they would be more than happy to try again, especially since I'm ovulating for sure."

So he said he'd call them and call me back if they did agree to come in. Well, two minutes later, the doctor called and told me to come in at 2:00 p.m. for the insemination.

I really felt the insemination was going to take that month but to my surprise, it didn't. I had mixed emotions at that point. I wanted to become pregnant, but then again I didn't, only because I hadn't talked with the father or his wife yet. I knew if I didn't meet them on my own at the doctor's office, chances of them being at the birth were almost impossible. I knew the lawyers weren't going to put any great effort into making it happen.

The next month I had to go for the inseminations on a Sunday and a Tuesday. On Sunday, I had to be there at 12:00 p.m. I took the boys with me and, as we pulled into the parking lot, there was one other car there. I noticed that someone was sitting in the car. I knew it wasn't the doctor's car and, since it was a Sunday, all the offices were closed. So who could it be but the father? I became a little nervous. This would be my chance to talk with him and get to know something about the couple. I said to myself, "Patty, just don't sit there, the doctor may come any minute—

then you'll never meet him. Get out of the car and see what he does." This is the chance I'd been waiting for, especially if I became pregnant this month. It was now or never! I got out of the car. The boys asked me if they could go for a walk. There was a creek near the parking lot and they wanted to sit by it.

We started heading towards the creek when I looked over at the father's car. He was out of his car and walking towards us. I asked, "Are you here to see the doctor?"

His reply was, "It isn't like we haven't seen one another before." I said I'd like to talk, if it was okay with him.

I explained how much I really wanted both him and his wife in the delivery room for the birth. The chances of the lawyer arranging it were almost impossible, since I usually go into labor in the middle of the night. At least, I did with my other two pregnancies. I didn't quite know how to ask him this next question. I asked him for their phone number so I could call them when I went into labor, and not have to rely on the lawyer. He said that was fine, as his wife wanted to meet me also. So we exchanged phone numbers so she and I could arrange to meet for lunch one day.

It was really nice talking to him. He told me a lot about his wife, why they chose Surrogate Mothering, and just things in general. Finally, I was finding out something about them. That was one thing I really had hoped for when I first got into the program. I knew if we didn't meet, I would always be curious. After giving birth and saying goodbye to the baby, I would always wonder who the parents were. Also, every time I saw a child, I would wonder if that was the child I carried for nine months. Now, knowing the parents, I wouldn't have any of those thoughts.

Just as we finished talking, the doctor pulled up—he was an hour late. We both got out of the car and John and the doctor went into the office. The boys and I waited outside for about ten minutes. As we went in the building and got into the elevator, I thanked God for giving me the chance to meet John, and also for allowing the doctor to be late.

I was excited that his wife, Sharon, was going to call me, and that we were going to meet one another. I couldn't wait to get home and call my husband to tell him what had just happened. My husband knew I had wanted to meet the couple, so he would be glad this was finally taking place.

My husband, John, was still down in Virginia, working on the house. He was getting much done. Every time I went down there, I couldn't believe the progress he was making. There were times when my 3-year-old went down and stayed with his dad for weeks at a time. That was really nice for John Matthew.

As little as he was, he learned a lot about house building. During that summer, he really did grow up and become very independent, especially since his dad was so busy working on the house all the time. John Matthew learned to do a lot for himself. I couldn't believe the things he did for a 3-year-old. The house was still in the raw stages. Think about it—no bathroom and no running water. They would take showers outside with gallons of water in plastic containers which they would let sit out all day to get warm from the sun. At night, they would stand on a platform my husband built, dump the water on themselves, soap up and rinse. They loved it! I didn't know if *I* would love it when I went down. How could I stand out there and take a shower that way? But I did, believe it or not! It wasn't as bad as I thought—in fact, it was nice to experience this new way of showering, with the mountains in the background and nothing around except the sun, trees and birds singing. I loved it!

John Matthew learned to make his own meals, which he did quite well. In fact, I prefer to have my son make my sandwiches now. He really does a great job! He never minded doing things for himself. He would work alongside his dad all day. I have some pictures of him using a hammer and nails on some wood and, when he got tired, down went the wood and he would use it for his pillow, no matter where he was. As young as he was, it was a great experience for him. First thing in the morning as soon as he opened his eyes, he'd say, "Come on, Dad—time to go to work." It wasn't until it got dark outside that he said, "Okay, Dad, time to quit for the day." Sometimes John Matthew would go to sleep at night with his clothes on, so he would be ready to work as soon as he got up the next morning. It was so cute.

I really missed him when he was with his dad but since I was working full time, it was better for him to be with his dad rather than with the babysitter. I enjoyed talking to him on the phone, and he would tell me all about his day.

Michael was still too young to know what was going on, so not being around his father or brother all the time didn't really affect him. It would be hard now for the family to be separated all those months, so I am glad we decided to build our home when we did.

When I got my husband on the phone the Sunday morning, after meeting the father in the doctor's parking lot, he was as pleased as I had been to learn something about John and Sharon. He wanted me to call him as soon as I heard from Sharon. He was such a big help— always sharing in my feelings and excitement!

It was 9:30 Monday morning when the

phone rang. Was it going to be Sharon? I picked up the phone and the girl on the other line said, "Hi, this is Sharon. Is this Patty?"

I said, "Yes, how are you? I'm really glad you called me."

I can't tell you which of us was more nervous, but despite this our conversation went well. We made arrangements to meet Thursday at 10:00 a.m. at a mall that was halfway between our homes—about an hour and a half ride for both of us.

The next morning was Tuesday and I had to be at the doctor's office again for the second insemination that month. This time as I walked into the office, not only were other women sitting there, but also John. It was a little strange for both of us to be sitting there waiting to see the doctor. As we started talking, I was thinking that here I was, talking with the man that, originally, I was never supposed to meet. I wonder what the nurses thought? I'm sure they became nervous, thinking we might find out about one another. Little did they know we already knew each other.

In the program, the lawyers and doctors try their best to keep confidential the identity of the couple and their Surrogate. I was glad the doctor didn't make it to the office on time that Sunday. Otherwise, I probably would never have met John and Sharon.

That day was the last time we were to meet at the doctor's office. After five months of inseminations, I finally became pregnant! John and Sharon were going to have their baby!

9

Meeting Sharon

I woke up about 5:00 in the morning and couldn't get back to sleep. I was too excited—it was the day I was to meet with Sharon! Since I couldn't sleep, I got out of bed and went through my closet trying to decide what to wear. About 7 a.m., I woke the boys to give them breakfast and get them dressed. They were going to their Mom-Mom's for the day.

Then I got dressed. I must have changed my outfit half a dozen times. Nothing seemed just right. I finally decided on a pair of jeans and a cotton blouse, which I had just bought.

I wasn't sure what Sharon would wear but, as it turned out, we were both in jeans.

It got to my mother-in-law's in plenty of time to sit and talk, before I left for the mall. It was nice to be able to leave the boys with Dulcie and Pearl, so I could spend time alone with Sharon. As I left the house, I kissed the boys and explained to them where I was going and how long I'd be. They were very good about staying with their Mom-Mom. In fact, she's about the only one they'll stay with for any length of time, besides my mom and dad.

I started towards the mall in my car. I was bubbling inside and couldn't wait to get there to see Sharon. I wanted to see what kind of woman she was, to see what she looked like, and just be able to talk to her about how she felt about me carrying her child. I also wanted to know what kind of things she expected of me while I was pregnant, and if there was anything I could do for her during the pregnancy. I wanted to make sure she knew exactly how I felt about being her Surrogate Mother. Then I realized I was already in the mall parking lot.

I parked the car. "What do I do now?" I thought. How was I going to know who Sharon was? I had no idea what she looked like. We were to meet at the entrance of Strawbridges, but no one was there yet! Should I go stand by the door just in case Sharon was already there, waiting for me to get there first? I decided it would be best for me to go to the entrance and wait. Besides, she knew what I looked like, so it would be easier for her to pick me out. As I got out of the car and was walking toward the door, I heard a voice calling my name. It had to be Sharon, I thought. I wasn't sure what I expected her to look like, but she was very attractive. She was about the same height and weight as myself, and our hair coloring was almost the same. As I looked at her, I knew I was going to like her. I felt we were going to get along great! I also felt we were already close friends and immediately felt comfortable around her.

We walked into the mall and decided to have a cup of tea. We found a small table where we could sit and talk. Sharon had been at the parking lot a half-hour early because she was nervous about being late, and I woke up at 5 a.m. because I was just as nervous. Now we were both laughing, not knowing which of us had been more nervous. We had a lot to learn about one another.

When we finished our tea, we walked around the mall, talking, shopping, and getting to know one another. It was close to

Christmas and we both did some Christmas shopping. It was really nice being with Sharon and learning things about her. We went into a clothing store and Sharon started to try some things on while I remained outside the dressing room. I stood there thinking how happy and fortunate I was to be able to meet the woman I was going to carry a baby for! I also thought how lucky Sharon was to be able to not think about maternity clothes and getting fat. She could still keep her trim figure. I couldn't wait to get pregnant for her.

When Sharon was finished trying on clothes we walked into another store. This time we looked at baby clothes, wondering if the baby would be a girl or boy. I asked Sharon what they wanted, a boy or girl? "It doesn't matter," she said, "as long as it's healthy." I felt so comfortable with Sharon that day it was like we had known each other for a long time and were the best of friends.

Little did we know, I was already two days pregnant when we met at the mall that day!

We discussed many different things that day, even the possibility that in eighteen years her son or daughter might want to meet me or my children. What would we do? We decided that we would contact each other first to see how we both felt. If we both agreed we would let the child know who I was and he or she could contact me.

Then we thought we'd eat lunch and call it a day. We both had an hour and a half drive so we started to look for a place to have lunch.

Over lunch, Sharon invited my family to their house to spend the day. She wanted us to meet their family and friends. I was excited she asked! By doing so, she was telling me she trusted me and knew exactly how I felt about being her Surrogate. I can't really say I'd have done the same thing. If I was in Sharon's shoes, I think I'd be a little afraid to let the Surrogate know where we lived, for fear she would always come around and want to be part of "our" family. But as the months went by and Sharon and I became close friends I know I would have done the same. It really depends on the persons involved. I feel Sharon and I are blessed to have had each other, so we could have made the situation turn out as well as it did!

I told Sharon I'd call John to see how he felt about us visiting and would let her know as soon as I could. After we finished lunch, we walked back to Strawbridges and said good-bye. As I watched Sharon walk toward her car, I had a big smile on my face and was feeling real pleased about our first meeting. Then I walked outside, got into my car and drove back to Pearl's to pick up the boys.

I was no sooner in the door when the questions came flying at me, "What was she like?

What did she look like? What did you talk about? Are you going to see her again?"

"Whoa—wait a minute!" I said. "Let me say hello to the boys and give them some kisses, then I'll sit and tell you all about it." I couldn't wait to see the boys. They were playing out in the back yard. It's nice to have time without them but boy do I miss them, even when it's only a few hours. When I think of that, I also think that, as a Surrogate Mother, I'm going to help another woman have a child. She will be able to feel for her child what I feel for my own children! That alone makes it all worth it.

The following week I made plans to spend the day at Sharon's house. My husband was still in Virginia, so it was just going to be me and the boys. It was almost a four hour drive so we left early in the morning and arrived there at noon. We met the couple at a diner about ten minutes from their house, went in and had lunch. It was a little awkward at first, but I was really glad to have the opportunity to spend more time with them. After lunch, we went back to their house. Sharon's sister and nephew stopped over and they were really nice. All of us went for a ride; they showed me the town and their place of business. Then we went out to their summer home on the lake.

The entire time we were riding around, I kept thinking, "What other Surrogate would find this out about her couple?" Another couple might be afraid to do this for fear that one day, in years to come, the Surrogate would come around looking for the child or to interfere in their lives. It gave me such a good feeling to know they had so much trust in me.

When we finally got back to their place, we ended up sitting in the kitchen talking. Sharon brought out something for us to eat, then gave me a tour of their house. It was very nice, and I felt good about being there.

A few of their friends stopped over, then Sharon's parents and sister. I do remember feeling a little strange at the time, wondering what everyone was feeling towards me. But that feeling soon left because they were all so friendly—they did nothing but make me feel perfectly comfortable. There were other children there, so my two boys had someone to play with. They spent a good part of the day outside, while we were inside getting to know each other.

It was a great day, but I finally had to leave, as we had a long drive home. I told Sharon I would call her Thursday or Friday, because I had to get a blood test to see if the inseminations took that month. She asked me if I felt pregnant. I couldn't say, because I never really knew—I never had morning sickness or felt any different. We would just have to wait until the blood test. We walked outside and said goodbye. Sharon then handed my sons each their own present—a coloring book and crayons. This thrilled the boys to death!

I headed home and, as I got on the turnpike, I thanked God for letting me meet the parents, and for helping me feel the way I do about Surrogate Mothering.

That Thursday I drove to the doctor's office for the blood test. I would find out the results the following day. I couldn't wait. I was hoping I was pregnant this time. After all, I knew the parents now, and we were both very anxious for the pregnancy to happen.

The next day I was at work when the doctor called. All he said was, "Congratulations, you're going to be a mother!" I wanted to scream and jump up and down for joy, but the girls I worked with would have thought I was really nuts!

I felt as though a special friend became pregnant after trying for ten years! I was so elated, I got tears in my eyes and wanted to run and hug Sharon—now to call and tell her! Too late, the doctor had just called and John and Sharon were both crying. They couldn't even talk to me. They didn't have to—I knew exactly how they were feeling! When I hung up the phone, the joy I felt was nothing like I've ever experienced before. I can't even describe it to you. I'm sure Sharon and I were both feeling the same way. I also felt that during the next nine months, Sharon and I were going to be one.

10

A Live Radio Talk Show

During the months of inseminations, I took my two sons with me on my visits to the doctor. My two-year-old was too young to realize what was going on, but my four-year-old had a lot of questions. He would always ask what the doctor was doing and why.

I tried my best to explain what was going on. After each insemination, before I left his office, I had twenty or thirty minutes to talk with him. I started by telling him how happy

I was to be his mommy, and how happy his daddy was to have two little boys like him and Michael. I tried to tell him there were some mommies and daddies who tried very hard to have little babies, but just couldn't. "That's why I am here at the doctor's office. I'm going to help a couple by carrying a baby in my belly until the baby gets big and strong enough to come out of my belly. Then I can give the baby to John and Sharon so they can be mommy and daddy to this little baby. They will love the baby just like your mommy and daddy love you and Michael."

I don't know how much he understood. When both our boys get old enough to really understand, my husband and I will sit down with them and tell them all about when I was a Surrogate Mother. I tend to believe John really did understand a lot at the time, because he would always talk about the baby in Mommy's belly as Sharon's baby.

One day the boys and I went over to a woman's house to look at maternity clothes she was selling. When I went into the other room to try them on, I could hear little John talking with her. I had to laugh when I heard the conversation. The woman was asking him if he wanted a baby brother or sister.

John said, "Oh, that's not my mommy's baby—we're going to give it to Sharon."

I almost fell on the floor laughing. I couldn't

believe he said that. I was really glad, though, that he talked about the baby as Sharon's baby, and not ours. I had to walk out and see what this woman was going to say to me. She said nothing. I looked at her and told her I heard the conversation, and that I guessed she was wondering what my son meant about the baby. I then told her I was a Surrogate Mother. The lady said she had wondered what he meant, but didn't know how to ask me. She really didn't say much after that, and didn't even have any questions. I guess she didn't think much of the idea, or maybe she knew very little on the subject.

I only had one other situation like that. Little John and I were shopping, and I started talking to another lady in the store. She asked me when I was due. I told her, in June. She had asked a few questions and I simply tried to answer the best I could without actually telling her I was a Surrogate, but without lying, either. I felt I would never see this lady again, so why go into the details? The conversation went very well, then we said goodbye.

Just as we were walking away, my son said, "You know, lady, it isn't my mommy's baby." I bet that woman is *still* wondering what he meant by that!

I found out during the pregnancy there are a lot of people interested in Surrogate Mothering, more than I originally thought. At first, I thought I would get more negative reactions than positive reactions, but to my surprise, I was wrong. I would say 98% of the reactions I received were positive! I'd like to share them with you.

Even before I became pregnant, I was on a live radio talk show with one of the lawyers. I had Michelle, a friend of mine, tape the show so I could play it for my parents. I thought that might help them understand more about Surrogate Mothering. The following Sunday after the show, I took the tape and a recorder over to my parents' house. I asked them to listen to the whole show before saying anything. Afterwards, we could talk about it. When the tape was over, they did have questions, to my surprise, and we talked for awhile. I think by the time I left, they felt more comfortable about me being a Surrogate and they had accepted it. I felt so much more at ease now that my parents had talked about it with me.

Others were interested in hearing about my experience of being a Surrogate Mother. I was asked to be on a live radio show in Philadelphia. The show lasted one hour. The subject, of course, was Surrogate Mothering and, at the time of the show, I had just been accepted into the program. At the end of the show, the host remarked that he wished he had made provisions for the program to have lasted two hours, because it went so well and he had so many people calling in to give their opinions on Surrogate Mothering.

I was so nervous sitting there waiting for the show to begin, that I was afraid to talk, for fear everyone would hear my voice shaking. However, the host was very friendly and helped me to feel comfortable. Within minutes, I was relaxed and anxious to talk on the subject of Surrogate Mothering.

Then he said, "4—3—2—1", and I realized that the show was on the air and live!

Host: We are now living in an age of technology that gives us the opportunity to give a couple a child that is at least biologically 50% theirs. What kind of woman would carry another man's baby? How much should she be reimbursed? What happens if, on the day the baby is born, the mother says, "That's my baby"? What happens if, in the course of the nine months, she says, "This is ridiculous! I've changed my mind—let's have an abortion"? How does it all work?

In light of the fact that one out of five or one out of six American couples are infertile and unable to have children, it's said that the most desperate people in the world are ones that have cancer and are looking for a cure, and the others are those who are trying to have children and can't.

Today on our show, we will be talking to two people—a lawyer with a Surrogate Mothering program and the other is a woman who is in the process of becoming a Surrogate Mother and is going to carry another man's baby. During the show, we will have a chance to get your questions and comments, but first, let's talk with our guests—the lawyer, whom we'll call Barbara, and the Surrogate Mother—we'll call her Pat.

Host: Pat, do you know anything about the man whose child you will carry for nine months?

Pat: Just that he and his wife are both in their early thirties, married for thirteen years and have been trying to have children for about ten years.

Host: Do you have any children?

Pat: Yes.

Host: How many and what are their ages?

Pat: We have two boys, one is four—the other is two.

Host: Are you married?

Pat: Yes.

Host: How does your husband feel about you carrying another man's baby?

Pat: He's all for it. He thinks it's great I can be a Surrogate Mother. It took us two years to conceive our first son, so we can both really understand how a couple must feel who cannot have any children.

Host: As close as you are to your own children, in this whole package, the hardest part for you will be what? Walking away from the baby?

Pat: No.

Host: How can a mother of two children say that?

Pat: Because I'm going into this program knowing when I do get pregnant, the child is going to be the child of another woman, because she cannot carry the baby herself. I feel I am just the "carrier" for this little baby, and not his mother. The couple that chose me already decided they wanted this baby and only needed me to carry him full term to be born as their child. In fact, when I give birth, I hope more than anything the couple will be able to be right there with me, so they can witness the birth of their child. I want the baby to be able to go right into his mother's arms and feel how much he is wanted.

Host: Barbara, the people that come to you, do they come because there's a problem with the woman?

Barbara: Yes, we only take couples where the husband's sperm count is normal and the wife is unable to conceive a child.

Host: Am I right in thinking that the people who come to you want their own children and are very desperate?

Barbara: That's correct, they are very desperate because, by the time they come to us, they've been through a lot. They tell us stories about the surgery the wife has gone through. Some of the couples have already gone through the procedure of adoption and are on the waiting list which is five to seven years long. They are very anxious about our program.

Host: What is the ball park figure that the Surrogate Mother receives?

Barbara: Just for the Surrogate, she gets anywhere from $7,500 to $13,000, depending on what she requests. We do have one Surrogate who requested $20,000, but she hasn't been chosen yet.

Host: What are the lawyer's fees?

Barbara: Somewhere around $10,000, which includes the medical, legal and psychological expenses.

Host: Can Pat change her mind during the course of the pregnancy?

Barbara: If she does, she breaks her end of the contract, and no longer is entitled to her fee.

Host: At what point will the child be separated from Pat?

Barbara: Right after the birth, the baby will be taken away.

Host: At what point will the adoptive parents be able to see the baby?

Barbara: As soon as he or she is taken to the nursery, the couple is able to see the baby.

Host: How is the money handled?

Barbara: The couple is required to put up seventy-five percent of the money at the time of signing the contract, then the balance is due when the Surrogate is four months pregnant.

Host: What's to keep the mother—ten years from now—taking the lawyers and the adoptive parents to court to find out where her baby is? Or even from wanting visitation rights? What is done to keep all this from happening?

Barbara: Thirty days after the birth, the Surrogate is required to terminate her parental rights. The Surrogate can change her mind legally. She cannot be forced to give up her child, but because she did sign the contract between herself and the adoptive couple, she cannot keep the child. If she does not agree to terminate her rights, the couple then has three options. They can choose to give the child to the Surrogate, pick a new Surrogate and start over again or they can proceed with a custody battle and let the judge determine what is the best interest for the baby.

Here are some questions and comments from our listeners. They were either directed to myself or to the lawyer.

A man called in just to comment on bonding. "I think the couple should definitely be there for the birth because there is a 'special bond' at that specific time for the parents and baby."

Both the lawyers and doctors didn't agree that bonding was necessary, they didn't feel that it was very important for the couple to witness the birth of their child. On the other hand, I feel it *is* important for the adoptive parents to be there, especially for the baby. I believe the baby can sense their presence and be aware of that special feeling of bonding.

A woman called in and asked the lawyer: "What is the effect on the wife of the natural father? And how does she really feel?"

Barbara: We have found that the wives are very anxious to participate in our program. They are the ones who have gone through all the different kinds of surgery and they are unable to have children of their own. They are very excited about becoming mothers, especially if the child is biologically her husband's.

Another woman called in to thank me for adding some dignity to this new service. I was glad she called in. It's nice to hear someone's positive reaction, especially after this next woman's comments. To this day, I still can't believe how this woman felt about Surrogate Mothering.

She started out by telling us she was adopted. It was very hard for her growing up and finally accepting the fact that she was adopted. "If I had known I was a Surrogate child, I wouldn't have been able to handle it at all! Especially knowing that I was so worthless, I had to be sold!"

My answer to her was that I felt Surrogate children are most definitely *not* being sold! She interrupted by saying, "You're getting money, aren't you?"

I tried to explain I was being paid for a service, not a child, but she just couldn't understand. I also tried to tell her that Surrogate children are more wanted than an adoptive child, because the couple decided to have that child, then looked for a woman to be their Surrogate. It's not like someone became pregnant by accident and then gave the baby up for adoption.

The host then asked her if she had children and she replied, "Yes, I love children very much."

Host: What if you had been in the position that you couldn't have any children of your own, wouldn't you adopt?

The woman: Definitely not! I'd go through life without them.

All I could say at that point was, "How sad it would be for someone who loved children to go through life without them, especially around Christmas and all the holidays."

Another caller said she felt that children shouldn't be told they were adopted, especially if the parents had them from birth. Their parents are their parents, regardless of who gave birth to them. She felt most adoptive children don't really want to seek out their biological parents.

The host disagreed. He felt that most adoptive children do seek out their biological mother just out of curiosity.

The next man who called in asked me if I considered myself a religious person, and how all this fit in with God's will.

I told him I did consider myself religious, and as far as God's will, God already gave me two beautiful children to love and raise, and to get all the joy from them that I do. Now, God is giving an infertile couple a child through me, because my body can carry and nourish this little soul until he or she is ready to be born to the parents. A mother is not necessarily the one who carries the baby nine months. A mother is the one who takes care of you twenty-four hours a day, changing diapers, feeding you when you're hungry, and comforting you when you're crying, whether it's for one hour or twenty-four hours. She is the one who would do anything in the world for you and is *always* there when you need her.

Now *you* decide who the mother really is! The woman who does all that or the woman who carries you for nine months?

The last caller was a man who parked his car near a phone booth to add to the conversation, "I think many people are really insensitive to the problem of infertility." He happened to be part of a couple with infertility problems, and *he* was the one who couldn't have children, not his wife. They were in the process of paying a man for his sperm to artificially inseminate his wife. "We are not looking for an adoptive child, we feel those children are 'unwanted' children. We feel better about going the route we chose or going through the program of Surrogate Mothering. Those children are more wanted; they are wanted even before they are conceived! People cannot imagine what a couple goes through when every one of their friends have children. Some even have two or three, and we can't have one!"

The program ended with his question, "Are parents who are fertile buying a child when they give doctors hundreds and sometimes thousands of dollars when they have a baby?"

This certainly gave the listeners something to think about and helped put the whole financial situation in better perspective.

11

People's Comments

The next tape I'm going to tell you about was pre-recorded and played on a radio talk show on a Sunday morning, which just happened to be "Mother's Day".

It started out with the lawyer, Barbara, saying they find, in general, Surrogates' families, husbands and friends are very supportive. Most of the Surrogates already have their approval before they enter the Surrogate Mothering program.

The host stated the one problem discussed most is whether or not the couple should tell the child he or she is the offspring of a Surrogate Mother. He also asked about the legal process for the adoption.

Barbara: Thirty days after the birth, the Surrogate goes to court to terminate her parental rights. Then six months after the birth, the couple goes through the formal adoption where the birth certificate is amended to read that the couple are, in fact, the parents of the child.

Pat: I feel an adoptive child is different from a Surrogate child, because at least the Surrogate child comes from his natural father and is living with him. An adoptive child does not know anything about his biological mother and father, and may tend to want to search more for his roots.

Host: Could this child search out his biological mother?

Barbara: No, the original records and birth certificates are impounded and it would be most difficult or almost impossible for the children to get their records.

The host then made the statement there are three million childless couples in the United

States and he feels that Surrogate Mothering will become a booming business.

Barbara said there is a great demand for Surrogate Mothers, and the ones in their program come from all walks of life. The women range in age from 21 to 37—and are students, housewives, business women, and lawyers.

Barbara: They want to become Surrogates for different reasons, but there are three factors that play a role in helping them decide to go into the program: 1. Financial consideration; 2. Feelings of sympathy for the infertile couple; and 3. They feel very satisfied when they are pregnant.

The host went on to say that the reasons why a woman would want to become pregnant—suffer with morning sickness and undergo emotional and psychological effects from childbirth, all with the intention of giving the child away—range from sympathy to joy and fulfillment. However, compensation also becomes the prime motive of a woman who considers becoming a Surrogate Mother.

Barbara: The adoptive parents agree on a financial compensation to the Surrogate, which usually covers potential loss of income, temporary suspension of relations with her husband and the pain and suffering with the risk of death.

Barbara: The fee that is paid to the lawyer usually covers the insurance, legal and medical costs.

Host: It might take some time before the whole idea of Surrogate Motherhood is accepted as normal and commonplace. The first babies born through artificial insemination made the headlines, but now there are around 10,000 such births a year.

Host: It may or may not be safe to conclude that in a relatively short time, Surrogate Motherhood may no longer shock our sense of what is normal and acceptable.

Here are some comments that were recorded before the day of the show, from people on the streets.

"I think it is a great program for an infertile couple who so desperately want their own children."

"Surrogates are doing a service which I believe is a good one, and they should get paid for it."

"A lot of people in the world can't have children and really want them. People like that would make great parents."

"People who try to adopt through an agency are put on a waiting list which is usually around five to seven years."

"If a woman wants to carry a baby for another woman and feels perfectly comfortable, then it's okay by me."

"I don't think a woman can carry a baby for nine months, then turn around, and give it up to the couple."

"Surrogate Mothering is definitely the right way; because if a couple can't have children on their own, they have to be able to have them some way. What better way to adopt than Surrogate Mothering, since the child is biologically the father's."

"I think it's up to the individual, if they choose to do it, then why not?"

"I think it is morally wrong. It is an intimate and personal thing and should only be shared between husband and wife."

At the end of the comments, the host began with his questions.

Host: What happens if a Surrogate Mother changes her mind after she has given birth?

Barbara: As it is now, there is no law actually stating the Surrogate must give up her parental right. The Surrogate and adoptive parents are pretty much trusting each other on their word.

Host: Barbara, people talk about Surrogate Mothering as baby selling, what is your feeling on this statement?

Barbara: This cannot be considered "baby selling". First of all, it would be very difficult to sell the child when, in fact, he or she is going to their biological father. Second of all, the Surrogate is being paid for her service, not a product.

The final part of the program is a discussion with a Monsignor who gives his views on the subject, along with the views of his church.

The Monsignor said the Catholic church believes a child ought to come from a marriage between a husband and wife and through an act of love between the two. He even remarked he knows not everyone would agree with his statement, but that is what the church believes.

Host: Assuming that a Catholic couple decided to contract with a Surrogate Mother to have their child, what would be the status of that child in the eyes of the church?

Monsignor: If the child is presented to the church and the parents want to have their child baptised, the church would want to know if the couple will, in fact, rear the child as a Catholic. The child will not be punished. It is still the responsibility of the parents to bring up the child, who is God's gift. If they want to bring the child up as a Catholic, the church would be very happy with that!

Monsignor: There's no way Surrogate Mothering can be altered so that the church could accept it. They suggest adoption as an alternative route to Surrogate Mothering. The church believes that the baby is a product and there would be problems if the baby were born abnormal. There would be a problem of knowing if the baby is actually the adoptive couple's or if, indeed, it is the Surrogate's husband's. Last of all, because of the money involved, Surrogate Mothering could become a big business.

The church is also concerned the child will want to look up his biological mother and I don't think any amount of negotiations can sever that relationship. In that sense, Surrogate Mothering is a real problem.

The lawyer concluded that there is a heavy strain on the Surrogate carrying the child nine months, and there is a great deal of selectivity involved in choosing a Surrogate Mother. There's unselfishness on the part of the mother, because any compensation she gets can never compensate for what she has done. As long as she realizes she has no ties with the baby, the Surrogate is doing a great service for the infertile couple.

The last statement from the host was: Throughout the program, we gave you some details on Surrogate Mothering and the ethical reflection on this subject. This crucial issue of the process of artificial insemination is still a growing concept. Since this is so, it is predictable that we shall see the rising of different arguments about whether Surrogate Mothering is tampering with nature or not. For example, we'll be forced with the question of whether or not Surrogate Mothering is unnatural and, therefore, is not a justifiable means of reproduction. However, it is perfectly understandable that no one would want to deprive a couple of the joy and fulfillment of having their own children. On the other hand, therefore, Surrogate Mothering seems to be a justifiable means of reproduction. One thing is for certain—the debate will continue for some time to come.

12

Live Television Show

I had received a letter from the lawyers asking me if I would like to appear on a live television program in Philadelphia, sometime in November. If I decided to do it, another Surrogate, the doctor and the lawyer were also going to be on the program.

The program was going to be on the same month my husband was coming home from Virginia. He was closing up the house for the winter and coming home to work, until after the baby was born sometime in June.

I had mixed emotions about appearing on a live television show. I really wanted to do it, so I could give my views and comments on Surrogate Mothering, as I could help some people understand a little more about the program. But there was the fact that people from all over our area would be watching and see me. I wasn't sure how my parents would like the idea of *everyone* knowing their daughter was a Surrogate Mother. Before I could decide what to do, I had to talk with my husband and my parents to see how they felt about it. As it turned out, my husband was going to be home the day before and said if I wanted to do it, it was fine with him. My parents really surprised me—they didn't mind at all. At this point, they had already accepted the fact that I was a Surrogate. In fact, the day the program was on, my mother had a television at work so she could watch the show.

The morning of the show, boy, was I nervous! I had to be at the studio by 9 a.m.—an hour earlier than the show began. My husband and boys dropped me off at the station, then went on to my mother-in-law's to watch the program on television.

I walked into the studio. Karen, the other Surrogate, was already there. They took us into a room to sign some papers and wait until it was time to go out on the set.

A girl came over to us and told us I would be on the first part of the show, with the host and hostess. After ten minutes or so, the lawyer and doctor would be introduced. During the last part of the show, they would bring in Karen. Why was I going to be the first guest? Did they know something I didn't? Did they like the way I answered their questions when they interviewed me over the phone prior to the show—or not? I didn't know and I was too nervous to ask!

Five minutes before the show started, they took me into the studio and put the mikes on me. As I walked out, there were so many bright lights and so many people sitting in the studio! They just stared at me. This made me feel a little uncomfortable at first, but I got used to them. I wasn't sure if they were for or against Surrogate Mothering. I guess I was about to find out!

When everyone was ready, the show began. I was introduced, and they asked questions about myself and why I wanted to be a Surrogate Mother. The host explained what Surrogate Mothering was all about, as well as some of the legal aspects.

After the commercial, the lawyer and doctor were introduced. They explained the legal part of Surrogate Mothering, along with the medical aspects. Toward the end of the show, Karen, the other Surrogate, was introduced.

Then we heard her views on the subject, and why she chose to be a Surrogate. I find that just about all women who decide to go into the program, enter for almost the same reasons. They know how an infertile couple feels, they have financial reasons, and they just want to do something rewarding for someone else.

Next, they asked for people to call into the studio with questions or comments, then went to the live audience for their comments.

One girl thought Surrogate Mothering was completely wrong. Another woman thought it was terrific for the couple to have someone like a Surrogate to help them bring their child into the world. Of course, there were some who looked at it like we were selling our babies. I didn't think they would understand how it must feel not to be able to have children of their own. I don't really understand how they can feel the Surrogates are selling their babies when, in fact, the children are being raised by their natural father! In my view, if it weren't for the infertile couple in the first place, the baby would never have been conceived!

To everyone's surprise, the first telephone caller was the father of Karen's baby! He started to explain how grateful both he and his wife were for Surrogate Mothering. He then was disconnected and never did call back. The host said he might have tried to call again, but they were having problems with the phone lines and maybe he wasn't able to get through.

Another man called in. He and his wife had just received their baby from their Surrogate. He was so ecstatic about the whole thing and wanted to tell everyone how he and his wife felt. As far as the money involved, he commented, "It's like having a second mortgage payment, but look what we have now! Something no one could ever put a price on!"

There were a lot of pros and cons during that hour. By the end of the show, I thought the people understood the Surrogate Program a little bit better. Some people even came up to me and said they were really glad they came to the show that day. They felt much better about the whole idea of Surrogate Mothering.

When I left the show, I really felt good. I felt we had changed some people's minds, but there were some women who would never approve of the program, no matter what you said. Overall, everyone concerned was pleased with the way the program went.

As I walked out, people smiled and nodded at me, as if to say, "I think what you're doing is a good thing." Just as I opened the door of the studio, onto the streets of Philadelphia, my husband came around the corner to pick me up. As we drove down the street, I was pleased I had decided to go on the show. I think it is a good program, and I liked expressing my views on Surrogate Mothering.

I don't expect to change anyone's mind about Surrogate Mothering. I just hope I can help people to understand more about the program and the reasons why it is an alternative way for infertile couples to adopt children.

13

Our Doubts

Almost a month had gone by now, and I hadn't heard a word from Sharon. I had begun to wonder why, when I finally got a phone call from her husband, John. I asked if everything was all right. He explained to me that Sharon was going through a tough time right now, but she did want him to call to see how I was doing. I tried to explain to John how I felt so he could tell Sharon. I wanted her to know exactly how I felt and I had no intention of keeping the baby! He told me that Sharon wanted this baby very much, and for me not to worry about anything.

After we hung up, I started thinking about what he said. I really could understand what Sharon was going through. I'm sure all she could think about at this stage of the pregnancy was whether or not I would be able to give up the child after carrying him nine months. I bet that is a very normal and natural question in this situation.

I'm sure another natural thought would be whether or not I would have a miscarriage. They are so common these days. After waiting for years, I'm sure Sharon worried about not being able to get this child. Just thinking about these things would really be hard to handle!

Sharon waited so long to be able to have this child. Now that it was actually going to happen, I guess it was hard for her to believe. Just to think, in nine months, she was actually going to see her baby, be able to hold him and take him home!

John told me that Sharon wanted this baby more than anything in the world, even though she wasn't quite ready to talk to me herself— not yet. All I wanted to do was to find a way to put all those thoughts out of her mind, so she could enjoy the pregnancy.

As the weeks went by, I started having some doubts about Sharon. What would I do if John and Sharon decided they didn't want this child! Where would that leave me? What if, God forbid, something happened to the father, would Sharon still want the baby? The longer I heard nothing from her, the more I thought about these possibilities. Finally, I couldn't wait any longer. I had to sit down and write a letter to her. I ended up with a four- or five-page letter, in which I told Sharon I wanted, more than anything, for her to feel a part of the pregnancy. If she could think of any way I could help her feel a part of it, to please let me know. I also told her of my fear that she might change her mind about wanting the baby. I explained why I chose to be a Surrogate Mother, how I felt about carrying another man's baby, and that I was very pleased to be their Surrogate and hoped that she felt the same way.

I told her I really needed to meet one more time to just talk. I mailed the letter, and prayed for an answer. But I only got phone calls from her husband, reassuring me that everything was fine, and Sharon would come around soon. I just had to give her more time. I wished Sharon would have called, so I could share things with her about the baby. I felt that she and I were part of each other during this special pregnancy.

Deep down in my heart I knew that, once the baby was born, everything was going to be fine. Sharon would feel like the real mother and all her doubts would disappear.

It was now time for another doctor's appointment. This time, he was going to give me an ultrasound. With the machine on my abdomen, he showed me the baby, then took a picture to send to John and Sharon. I couldn't tell it was the baby, as I was only twelve weeks pregnant. I couldn't even believe the doctor knew what he was looking at. To me, it didn't look much like anything. He said the baby was doing fine and growing just like he should be.

As I rode home, all I thought about was Sharon. It seemed that's all I ever thought about lately—John and Sharon. I decided I had to call her. I just *had* to tell her about the ultrasound. The minute I walked into the house, I picked up the phone and dialed— before I had time to change my mind. I was real nervous, but I had to talk with her. I wasn't even sure she would talk to me, or what she would do when she heard my voice. Would she hang up? I sure hoped not. To my relief, when she answered the phone, she acted as though nothing were wrong. I didn't regret calling. I told her about the visit to the doctor, the ultrasound, and that the doctor was going to send them the picture of the ultrasound.

She told me she had received my letter, and wanted to have lunch with me another time. She reassured me she wanted the baby more than anything in the world—that it was all she thought about now.

Since it was winter time, Sharon said she would prefer to meet when the weather was warmer. There was a lot of snow and ice, and Sharon didn't want to drive all that distance in it. I didn't mind—I was happy she wanted to see me again. We made plans to call each other in a few weeks. When the weather changed, we would meet again at the mall.

14

Hospital Policy

I had one more visit with the doctor who inseminated me, then I had to start going to my own doctor. The doctor who does the inseminations doesn't deliver the baby, so they send you to someone else for the remainder of your pregnancy.

At the time I signed the contract, I told the lawyers I very much wanted to go again to the woman doctor who delivered my other two children. I had already discussed it with her, and she was waiting for my call to tell her it was all right. The lawyers agreed to this arrangement.

To my surprise, when I discussed it with the doctor at our last visit, he said he didn't particularly care for the hospital my doctor worked with—for reasons he didn't want to get into. He said he would pick a doctor for me to see and also the hospital that I would be in. In a nice way, I told him I wanted *my* doctor and hospital, because I knew for sure that John and Sharon would both be allowed in the delivery room with us. We went back and forth on the subject and finally, I told him I would only consider going to someone other than my own doctor, if he could find another doctor and hospital that would allow both John and Sharon to be with me. So, during the next few months, I also called all the hospitals in the area to find out if they would allow this.

One hospital said their policy was that the only person allowed with me in labor and delivery had to be my husband. They could make no exceptions. Scratch *that* hospital from my list! Another hospital was exceptionally nice. The woman I talked to said she would try her best to have an exception made, since I was a Surrogate Mother. She asked a lot of questions and even went to some board meetings to try and make the hospital see this was an unusual, but very good, request. After about two months, she finally got back to me. She said she was very sorry, she had tried her best for us, but they would only allow one person in labor and delivery. It could have been either the mother, the father, or my husband, but not all of them. That wasn't good enough for me. Sure, I wanted my husband with me, but I also wanted the parents with me too! So *another* hospital was checked off my list.

Now I was truly getting annoyed at having to call all these different hospitals, explaining who I was, and asking what their policies were. I thought, "Why should I be doing all this? The lawyers already agreed I could see my own doctor. Here I am, calling all these hospitals, and for what? I didn't even want to go to any other doctor in the first place!"

Besides, three months had passed and I wasn't seeing any doctor at all. At this stage, I felt I should be seeing one. So I called the doctor one last time. I explained I couldn't find a hospital that would allow both John and Sharon in the delivery room with me and my husband. I said that I wanted to see my own doctor, since she would allow the four of us to be together for the birth.

Instead of agreeing, he told me I could go to the hospital where he was on staff, and to a doctor there. He would make the arrangements with him to allow John and Sharon to be with me.

I was really annoyed at this point and said, "Look, I have two boys at home. I have to worry about getting them to my mother-in-law's house when I go into labor. She lives too far away from your hospital, and besides, it's terribly inconvenient for me. If I go to the hospital I want, everything will be a whole lot easier for me."

I couldn't believe his next statement, "Patty, don't worry about the boys. If I have to come over to your house and take them to your mother-in-law's, I will."

Now, I knew that when the time came, the last thing he wanted to do was to drive 45 minutes over to my house, pick up my boys, drive another 35 minutes to my mother-in-law's, and then drive another 50 minutes to the hospital to deliver the baby!

I said, "Doctor, my boys will be uncomfortable going with you. They won't want to go with you when the time comes. Besides, *I* want to be the one to drop them off at my mother-in-law's. Would you *please* be reasonable!"

Finally, he said I could go to my own doctor. As soon as we hung up, I called her to make an appointment. I was so happy that she was going to deliver this baby—I couldn't wait to see her!

15

Losing My Job

Now I was three months pregnant and going through some changes at work. I worked full time in a beauty salon with three other girls. I really enjoyed my work intensely, as well as the girls I worked with. We got along really well. However, it seemed as though things changed a little when my pregnancy started showing. They would always talk to me about being a Surrogate. They were always asking, "Are you sure you're going to be able to give up the baby?"

No matter how much I tried to tell them how I felt—that the baby wasn't really mine in a sense—they still asked the same question. I tried to explain I was pregnant only because of John and Sharon. If it weren't for them, I wouldn't be carrying this child at all. But they just couldn't understand.

One girl in the shop was also trying to become pregnant. We used to talk all the time, but it seemed like when I did get pregnant, she didn't have much to say to me anymore. I had a feeling that she didn't like the idea of me being a Surrogate Mother, getting pregnant so easily, then turning around and giving the baby to another couple. This was probably why our conversation became so reserved. I could feel a lot of tension around the shop. At times I thought about leaving, but I enjoyed my work too much, and decided to stick it out.

Well, one night, in about my fourth month, my boss called me at home. She told me that business was really slow, and with the baby coming, she thought it better if I didn't come in anymore.

I was somewhat surprised, but I had felt that something like that was going to happen. After I hung up, I started wondering—was I laid off because the shop was slow, or because I was a Surrogate Mother? We dealt with the public all the time. When customers asked me about being pregnant, I didn't think twice about telling them the truth. I think that upset my boss to some degree. She never said anything to me about it—I just had this feeling. I was relieved in a way, now I could go look for another job. But then, who would hire someone who was pregnant?

The next day I went into work to collect my things. It was strange to go in and talk with the others because I wasn't sure what they thought about me leaving. Did my boss tell them she had called me the night before? And did she tell them why she laid me off?

I think the real reason she laid me off was because of an incident at work. One day, a customer asked me if I was pregnant. I told her the whole story. She was excited for me, and also for the couple. As soon as she was finished drying her hair, she ran over to my boss and started telling her how great she thought it was that I was doing this. And how beautiful it was that there are some people in the world who would do this for another couple.

My boss didn't have too much to say. In fact, her only response was, "If Patty can do it, fine, but *I* could never do it." Then she changed the subject.

I got my things together and said goodbye to the girls. One girl that I got along with well, told me to keep in touch with her, and to stop in whenever I was in the area.

When I got home, it was good to have all this time on my hands and to be able to do some things I normally couldn't because of my work. It felt great! It gave me a lot of time to think about the house we were building down in Virginia, and all our friends there. John and I hadn't planned to go down to the house anymore until the baby was born, because we didn't have the time. We really never thought of telling our friends about my being a Surrogate Mother. But if I didn't tell them, I just wouldn't feel comfortable about it. They were going to be our friends for many years to come, and I didn't want to have any secrets.

In the back of my mind, I kept thinking, "One night, twenty years from now, we'll be having all our friends over. Someone will knock on the door—I'll open it, and John and Sharon's child will be standing there. And of course, all our friends will ask who he was!"

When my husband came home that night, I told him I really wanted to tell our friends in Virginia. John could understand that, so we made plans to go down that coming weekend.

We arrived there Saturday morning and I was both a little nervous and excited about everything. As we were riding in town, we saw two of our real close friends so we stopped the truck to talk to them. John and Ruth came over to the door and invited us over for dinner that night. They were spending the afternoon house hunting. I was glad not to talk right then but I felt a little awkward because I didn't jump right out and give both of them a big hug. I would explain everything when we saw them at dinner.

Then we went to see Carla and her husband. As we walked in, they saw my belly and instantly realized what I had done. For the past few months I had been talking on the phone to Carla about Surrogate Mothering. While she didn't think it was a good idea for either me or the child, she did tell me, that Saturday morning, my decision to become a Surrogate Mother would not alter our friendship—I was still her good friend and nothing would change that!

We had dinner that evening with John and Ruth as planned. Ruth is going to tell you about her feelings in a later chapter.

I was so glad John and I decided to go to Virginia to tell our friends. The more friends we told, the better I felt!

16

Other Surrogate Mothers

It was March now, and my belly was growing bigger. Back in November, during my last visit with the doctor who inseminated me, I was told to come back in March for our final visit—just to make sure everything was going well. So here I was, in his office. When the doctor walked in, he asked me how I was doing. I looked at him a little awkwardly. I thought he was going to examine me or at least weigh me and take my blood pressure.

He didn't—he just asked how I was doing. I told him I was feeling good, and that everything was going fine.

He said, "Good—I guess I'll hear from you when you have the baby."

I couldn't believe it! I had to ride all the way up there for a "social visit", as the doctor put it. He said that's what it was, so he could tell the parents everything was fine with me and the baby. Well, we could have done that on the phone! It would have saved me a lot of time.

The following week, I had my monthly visit and checkup with my regular doctor. I was so glad to see her. I really liked her and thought she was a fantastic doctor! She was so flexible about how I wanted my birth to go. I think if we had asked her if my husband could deliver the baby, she would have agreed—just as long as she was there in case anything went wrong.

After she checked the baby's heartbeat, she told me she wanted me to meet someone. Her name was Susan and she was the head person in charge of the maternity unit at the hospital. My doctor explained our situation to her— that I wanted the couple in the birthing room with me, and they also wanted to be there. Susan wanted to meet me, in order to get more information so she could make all the necessary arrangements beforehand. I went to meet her after my appointment. She was very nice, and seemed to think she could make all the necessary arrangements. I told her how much I wanted John and Sharon with me, and how important this was to all of us. She asked me if they planned to feed the baby the two or three days he was in the nursery.

I said, "If I know them, they will be at the hospital twenty-four hours a day until they can take their baby home!"

She then said she would make sure the emergency attendants knew they would be coming in to witness the birth, so she could send them upstairs right away. She would also try to get John and Sharon a private room in which to feed their baby rather than feed him in the nursery. I thought that was really nice of Susan. How glad I was to come back to my own doctor, and the same hospital where I delivered my other two children! And I was thankful the hospital was going to go along with everything we wanted, and more.

After we finished talking, she told me to call her if I thought of anything else. If not, she would be coming to see me when I delivered the baby.

I got home and started thinking how nice it was to have all this time off. I got to do so many more things I wouldn't have been able to do because of working. I liked to keep in touch with Ms. Pazdan, one of my high school teachers. She taught my favorite subject— physical education. It seemed like every time

I went to see her, I was either pregnant or had a newborn in my arms.

It was the end of March when I decided to go see Ms. Pazdan again. She now taught at the Maple Shade High School which is only a few blocks from my parent's house. When I walked into the school and down the halls toward her office, I wondered what she would think about me being a Surrogate Mother. As soon as Ms. Pazdan saw me, I didn't need to explain. She already heard what I was about to do. I sat down and started talking, because we only had a few minutes before she had another class to teach. She asked me what I was doing the rest of the day, and if I had time to stay a few hours. She asked if I would be interested in talking with one of her senior classes on the subject of Surrogate Mothering. What would I say? I never talked in front of a class before! She told me just to explain what I was doing, how I became a Surrogate Mother and all the legal procedures. I thought —why not, maybe the students would have a lot of questions and that would make it easier. I agreed.

Most of the questions were asked by the guys, who seemed more interested than the girls. The girls had mixed feelings. Some felt they could be Surrogate Mothers without any problems. Others said they didn't believe anyone could carry a baby nine months, then turn around and give it up for adoption. There were also a lot of questions about the legal aspects, and about the money. Who paid for all the medical bills? What would happen if I changed my mind? What would happen if the couple decided they didn't want this baby? Would I see the baby once he was born?

One student asked me if I would come back next month. By that time, he would have time to think and write all his questions down. My teacher thought the class went really well. She was surprised there were so many questions—and that they were asked by the guys. We said goodbye, and she reminded me to keep in touch and let her know how the birth went.

Ms. Pazdan now tells me that I am part of their regular curriculum at the Maple Shade High School. When I was a Surrogate, Ms. Pazdan cut articles out of the local newspaper. She ended up saving them and now her classes discuss the subject of Surrogate Mothering. She said the students are real receptive and have lots of questions.

A few weeks later, the secretary in the lawyer's office called to ask if I would talk with a girl who was about to be inseminated. She was interested in talking with a Surrogate who either was pregnant or who had already given birth. She wanted to talk to someone before she was inseminated for the first time. I said I would be happy to. The secretary gave me her number, and I called her. We made plans for her to come to our house for lunch on Friday. Her name was Lois. The day she came over, she brought her son, who was two years old. The boys played in the yard while we talked.

Apparently she had mixed emotions and also many questions. It seemed as though she was having second thoughts about carrying someone else's baby. She also felt bad about letting the couple down that chose her if, in fact, she did decide to drop out of the program. She also told me she wanted to know who the parents were, so she could keep in touch with them after the baby was born.

I didn't think that was a very good idea for Lois, not after talking with her. It sounded as though she would always want to know what "her" baby was doing and where her baby was. I didn't want to give her any advice to influence her decision. All I could tell her was how I personally felt about being a Surrogate Mother, and my reasons for going into the program.

Being a Surrogate was a decision that only Lois could make. I feel that the decision has to be yours and yours alone. You have to be 100 percent sure it is something you really want to do, and not just for the money involved. I believe if you do it only for the money, it would be very hard to handle, both mentally and emotionally. There's more involved than the money, and I don't really think the money would change your true feelings. Please examine *all* the facts about Surrogate Mothering *before* you go into the program. I think you have to want to do it, not just for yourself, but also for the other people involved.

I did keep in touch with Lois. As of today, she has decided to drop out of the program. I was pleased to hear that. I believe if she had become pregnant, everything would have been pretty tough for her to handle—the nine months of pregnancy, and giving up the baby. If she did give up the baby when she left the hospital, she would have to go to court to give up her parental rights, which would have been still harder for her.

I did hear one story about another Surrogate Mother who gave birth. She insisted on feeding the baby while in the hospital. Everything went fine, until the third morning, the nurses didn't bring the baby to her. The Surrogate went to the nursery to find out why. They told her the parents had come that morning to take the baby home—she broke down. Emotionally, she couldn't handle the fact that they took "her" baby. She had a hard time accepting she had to give the baby up for adoption and that she was, in fact a Surrogate Mother, and not the real mother. I feel that it depends upon the individual woman as to whether or not they should spend time with the baby after they give birth.

In an effort to minimize the psychological and emotional anguish, the Surrogates are not supposed to see the babies after they're born, according to the program's guidelines.

But one Surrogate, Joanne, insisted. "I had wanted her parents there the minute she was born. I feel every baby needs a mother. But I was told they would not be allowed in the hospital until the day they took her home because of the adoption procedures. The nurses were absolutely fantastic, but a nurse is a nurse and a mommy's a mommy—so I decided that if I could handle it, I should do it."

Joanne spent three days in the hospital with the baby. "I got to feed her, change her and hold her. I wouldn't recommend that for every Surrogate, but I was so very glad I had that time with her."

Joanne did not cry when she said goodbye to her daughter in the hospital nursery, but she did cry the morning the baby was born.

"I cried because all the motherly love I felt for her the whole nine months naturally came out—I was just thrilled that she was so pretty and healthy. I didn't cry because I didn't want to give her away. I cried because I was so pleased."

17

Starting A New Job

The birth was getting closer now, as the weather became warmer. I decided to call Sharon, and find out when it was best for us to meet again for lunch. I always felt good talking with her, as there was such a strong bond between us. We set a lunch date for the first week in May, almost four weeks away.

In the weeks that followed, I looked for a full-time job, since John was going back down to Virginia to finish the house after the baby was born. I was staying here with the boys until after the house was ready for us to move in.

One day I got a phone call from a man who worked at a trucking company. He said he heard I was looking for a temporary job, and asked if I could come in for an interview that afternoon.

As I rode over to the office, I thought, "With my big belly, this guy will probably take one look at me and wonder why on earth someone 8½ months pregnant would be looking for a job.

When I walked into the office, did he look at me! Before he could say anything, I told him I was a Surrogate Mother. I said that I only planned to take two or three days off while I was in the hospital having the baby. I assured him I didn't need any more time off than that, and I was very interested in both the job and working full time. He said that was fine. Then he asked when I could start. I couldn't believe I got the job! The pay was a lot better than I made as a hairdresser, and the income would help John and me, since he was building our house and not working at his job.

I told him I could start Tuesday, if that was okay with him. I had already made plans to have lunch with Sharon on Monday and I really didn't want to cancel my meeting with her. That was fine with him—he said he would see me Tuesday.

I couldn't wait for John to get home from work. He wasn't even aware I was going for an interview that day. When he came home, I told him I just got a job making $358.80 a week, starting on Tuesday. He couldn't believe it. Most girls quit their jobs toward the end of their pregnancies, but I had just accepted one! Nothing I ever did surprised my husband—he knew me too well by now. He just shook his head and smiled at me.

Two nights later, I had a hard time sleeping. I was too excited about meeting with Sharon. Our lunch date was the next morning. It had been a few months since I last saw Sharon— my belly was really growing. How would she feel about seeing me so pregnant? Would this meeting go as well as our first one? I really hoped so!

And it did! When we met each other at the mall, Sharon had a big hug for me and the baby. We found an empty bench in the mall, and talked. I started by telling her how I felt when I gave birth to my own children. I went on to tell her that if I decided to keep this baby, I knew it would be no different for her than if someone had come into the birthing room when I gave birth to John and Michael, and told me they were going to take them away from me! I knew if I decided to keep this baby, I would be doing the same thing to Sharon. How could I live with myself? I think it was then she realized how I felt, and believed I had no intentions at all of keeping the baby.

Sharon then told me about all the operations she had. The more surgery she had, the more scar tissue she got. She was happy I was doing this for them, but she did have other feelings, which were only natural. "Sometimes I just wish I could be the one carrying the baby."

The rest of the day went great. Sharon ended up buying a little bear planter for the baby's room. She told me she couldn't go *anywhere* anymore without buying something for the baby.

While having lunch, we talked about being together for the birth. We were both really excited about the idea and hoped, when the time came, Sharon and her husband would both make it to the hospital on time. That day Sharon told me she had seen me once at the doctor's office.

"Really?" I said. "When?"

It had been at the very beginning of the inseminations, even before the day I ran into her husband. Sharon drove to the office with John. When he went into the office, Sharon waited outside the building. She was standing outside the door when she saw me pull up, get out of the car, and walk into the building. I must have walked right past her. I vaguely remembered seeing her, but I didn't realize who she was.

When we finished lunch, we walked out to the entrance and said goodbye. Sharon hugged me and said, "Take care of yourself, and of course, my kid." We both smiled and walked to our cars.

18

The Last Weeks

The next day, I started my new job. It was a one-woman office, so I didn't have to explain about the pregnancy. I really enjoyed working, because it made the days go by fast.

I talked with Sharon every week now, sometimes more. We both were too anxious because we felt the baby would be born early. Those last few weeks really were intense! I was excited about giving birth and excited that John and Sharon were going to be there with us. Most of all, I felt so happy all the time, always smiling and always in a good mood. Pretty soon, I was going to give something as precious as a little baby to two very special people!

One day I went into the camera shop where my parents get their film developed. The woman there said how great she thought it was I was a Surrogate Mother. I asked her how she knew. She told me that the other week my dad came in and she said to him, "I guess you'll be taking a lot of pictures of the new baby coming."

My dad said, "No, I won't be taking any at all." The woman was a little taken aback by his comment, so he continued, "My daughter's a Surrogate Mother."

I was really surprised to hear that my dad told her about me, but I was glad he did. Now I knew he was comfortable with the fact. He accepted it enough to tell someone and not be ashamed.

Then, I ran into a girl my father works with. She proceeded to tell me about a conversation she had with my dad. They were talking about me, and my dad made a comment, "Hey, will this make me a Surrogate Grandfather to the baby?" I thought that was really cute, and, knowing my dad the way I do, that is definitely something he would say.

One day, I stopped over at my gram's house. I missed her now I was working full time. When I was off, I went over almost every day with the boys to have lunch with her. When I walked in, she had friends of hers there. They told me they wished I had been around twenty years ago, when their son and his wife decided to adopt their children. He and his wife would have loved to have a Surrogate Mother carry their children for them—then at least the baby would have been half theirs, biologically.

I was now in the last week of the pregnancy, and a few of my good friends started getting really concerned about me. I don't think they fully understood what I was feeling. If they *did* understand, they wouldn't have had so many questions. Everyone was telling me how hard it was going to be to give up this baby I had been carrying for nine months. Then they would ask me if I was going to see the baby after he was born. I told them, yes, I was going to see the baby. The parents were going to be there with us and I was sure they wouldn't take him and go into another room immediately after he was born. Besides, I did want to see him, especially when he was placed in his parents' arms!

As far as giving him up—I wasn't giving him up like they thought. I was giving him to his natural father and his wife. She, in my eyes, was rightfully the baby's mother. If it weren't for both of them, this baby wouldn't be coming into the world.

Now that I was getting closer to having the baby, my grandmother was becoming somewhat sad. I could tell, every time I went to see her. She asked me if I would take a picture of the baby in the hospital, so she could see him. She really thought I should, but I told her I probably would not. I think she was disappointed.

Sharon and I would talk with one another on the phone almost every night now. I was getting a lot of contractions, but nothing steady or strong enough to know the baby was ready to be born. I always told her, "Nothing yet, Sharon, but maybe tonight or tomorrow."

The Sunday before the baby was due, Sharon called to tell me she was going swimming at the lake. She gave me the telephone number of the house and said to call if anything was happening with the contractions. Later, she told me every time the phone rang, she ran like crazy to answer it, thinking it was time to see the birth of her son.

The baby was due on Thursday. It was now Tuesday night. Sharon and I both thought for sure the baby was going to be born early. But here John and I were, on Tuesday night, sitting in our living room. I started to tell him that the contractions were starting to get stronger. They were still far enough apart, however, so it wasn't time for me to go to the hospital.

I thought, "Maybe tonight!"

We called Pearl and Dulcie to tell them what was going on. They had planned to take the boys while I was in the hospital, and the more we talked, the more I thought I would be going into labor that night. My sister-in-law said, "Why don't you bring the boys over now, just in case you end up going into labor in the middle of the night?"

So my husband and I packed their bags and took them over. We also took my hospital bag, just in case I went into labor while riding over there. When we got to my mother-in-law's, the contractions were still strong but not enough to go to the hospital, so John and I came home. By 11:00 p.m., nothing had happened, so we went to bed. To our surprise, morning came—with no interruptions.

The alarm went off and we just looked at one another. "Oh well, I guess the baby isn't ready yet." We then got ready for work.

As John walked out the door, I yelled, "Who knows, honey, maybe I'll call you at work to meet me at the hospital."

He laughed, "I doubt it, Patty, I bet I'll see you for dinner tonight." I laughed too and thought he was probably right.

As I got ready for work, I felt strange not to have to get the boys ready to go to the babysitter. Boy, did I miss them—and they had only left the night before! As soon as I got to work, I called to talk with them. They were having a good time and I don't even think they missed us. They always enjoyed going over to their Mom-Mom's and Aunt Dulcie's.

By lunch time, I started getting contractions again. This time, they were pretty steady, but only fifteen to twenty minutes apart. I tried to call my doctor to see if she was home. She had given me her home number, because she was on vacation that week. She had said she would only be going on day trips, and for me to try and reach her when it was time for the baby to be born. Otherwise, her associate would deliver the baby. I really wanted my doctor to be in town. I liked her very much and trusted her, and I wanted, more than anything, for her to deliver this baby. When I called her home, somebody else answered and said she would be back late that night.

So, I went back to work and tried to keep my mind off the contractions—maybe they would go away. By 5:00 p.m., it was time to go home, and the contractions were still there. I told my boss I had a feeling I'd be calling him from the hospital the next morning to tell him I wouldn't be able to come to work. He said fine, if I didn't show up, he would know that I had had the baby.

I walked in the house. John was already home and had our dinner all cooked and on the table. Boy, was that nice! I really didn't feel much like cooking. After all, I was in labor, even if it was the early stages.

It was nice for just the two of us to have dinner together. But, I have to admit, John and I both missed the boys. I had even suggested going over to get them. But I knew I couldn't, not with the contractions the way they were—this baby was going to be born sometime tonight. And why not? The due date was the following day!

That night, right after dinner, a customer called to see if I could give her a permanent. I thought, "Why not?" If she came right over, I had two hours to do it. John just looked at me, smiled, shook his head and said, "I don't believe you, Patty! If you think you should, go ahead."

I was in the middle of the perm when the phone rang. It was Sharon, wondering what was happening with the baby. I told her what was going on, and that I had a feeling I would be calling her in the middle of the night. I asked if she had her bags packed. She assured me that she did, and that she had been ready for *weeks*!

19

The Birth

It was 1:15 a.m. when I woke up with strong, heavy contractions. *This* time they were close together! I tried to go back to sleep but, because of the pain, I couldn't. I got out of bed and walked into the living room to get the stopwatch. I wanted to make sure this was the real thing before waking John or calling Sharon, so I sat on the sofa with just a dim light on in order to see the stopwatch. I started timing my contractions and getting excited that it was finally time for Sharon's baby to be born. I couldn't wait to call her. But still I sat there timing the pains and wondering if this was it. They were now getting stronger and closer together but still I sat there.

I timed them for almost an hour and a half. They were steady five minutes apart—now I knew they were the real thing! But before I woke John, I called my doctor's house, just past 2:30 a.m. She was half asleep, but all I thought was, "She's home!" I told her my contractions were five minutes apart. She explained to me that she was going out of town again the next morning. If I wanted her to deliver the baby, it had to be *now*! So I agreed to meet her at the hospital.

I went into the bedroom to wake John and told him it was time to go to the hospital. The contractions were now extremely strong. As John was getting ready, I called Sharon. Her husband answered and I was so excited I wasn't sure what to say. Then Sharon got on the phone—all I could say was it was time for the baby to come. They had a three hour drive, so I suggested they drive halfway and call the hospital to make sure they admitted me.

Sharon said, "No, we can't take the time to stop—we may miss the birth. We'll see you at the hospital!"

As soon as I hung up, we grabbed our bags,

my gifts for the new mother, and were on our way!

At 3:10 a.m., we arrived at the hospital, and told the woman in emergency that another couple would be coming to be in delivery with us.

She said, "I already know. As soon as they get here, I'll send them right up."

Within seconds, someone brought a wheelchair around the corner, and up to the maternity unit I went! As I was wheeled through the doors, there stood the midwife who delivered Michael, as well as a nurse I had when John was born. They were arm-in-arm with each other, and had great big smiles on their faces.

When I had called the hospital to tell them I was on my way, I asked if the birthing room was available. I was told someone was already in there, but I could use one of the labor rooms to deliver the baby. I was disappointed because, with John and Sharon being there, I thought the birthing room would really be nice for them. To my surprise, the midwife and nurse moved the woman who was in it, so we could use it. They explained to me she wasn't in labor yet, and they had asked her if she would mind moving into another room. After she heard about our circumstances, she was more than happy to let us use the birthing room.

It was really a nice room—it almost made

you feel like you were at home in your own bedroom. There was a sofa, stereo, television, and of course, a telephone. It was very cozy and was just the perfect place to give birth.

I was on the monitor for a little while just to watch the baby's heartbeat and also the contractions. They were now two minutes apart. We were all hoping the parents would make it on time for the actual delivery. At that moment, the phone rang. It was someone from the emergency room saying that John and Sharon were on their way up.

You can't imagine how I felt! When I think of it now, I still get tears in my eyes for the joy I felt and still feel. At 5:00 a.m., they walked in, with the contractions just two minutes apart. I introduced my husband, John, to Sharon and her husband, John. They sat down on the sofa which was across from the birthing bed.

I sat there and looked at them, thinking how happy I was to be there, about to give birth to their child. How happy I was going to make John and Sharon when I delivered the baby! I was so glad they were able to witness the birth, and I thanked God for letting everything happen as it did.

Around 5:30 a.m., my doctor walked in with some papers to sign. She started asking me and the father questions. She wrote everything down, then the two of us had to sign. I felt awkward at first, but everything went so smoothly, it just seemed right. It was as though the four of us were all good friends and had known each other a long, long time.

At 6:00 a.m., the door opened and in walked my doctor again. This time the nurse was with her and they were pulling their gloves on.

"What are you doing?" I asked.

They looked at me and said, "It's time for the baby!"

I couldn't believe it, I only had a few really hard labor pains. I had just told my husband I really didn't feel like I was in hard labor and wondered why the pains weren't stronger.

The doctor got me in position to deliver and told me to start pushing.

Start pushing? I didn't even feel ready yet, but I wasn't going to say anything. After all, she was the doctor and knew best. So I started to push. About twenty minutes went by and nothing was happening. The baby's head kept crowning as I pushed, but wouldn't stay there. I started to feel something was wrong, and soon realized I was right when I looked at my doctor's face. I asked her what was the matter.

At first she said, "Everything is fine. Just try and push harder so we can get the baby out."

So I tried my hardest—but still the baby wasn't coming. I looked at my husband and started to get real concerned.

He just looked at me and held my hand even tighter. "Come on, honey, try and push harder, everything's going to be fine."

It was then the doctor told me they were going to take me down the hall to the delivery room, to use suction to get the baby out. John and Sharon looked upset. We both had no idea what was wrong. Then another doctor went over to them, and explained that the baby had meconium, and it was best if the baby could be born as soon as possible. They even had to call a pediatrician, just in case something was wrong with the baby when he was born.

They put the sheet over my legs and started to move me off the bed when I said, "Let me try again to push. Please!"

My husband looked at me and said, "Patty, you really don't want to go into that delivery room. It's so impersonal. *Please*, put all your energy into pushing—just visualize the baby coming down the birth canal."

· He was right—I didn't want John and Sharon to experience the birth of their baby in that room, so I told the doctor I had to push one more time before we left.

She said okay, and just held her hand over the sheet. She didn't even bother to remove it. As I pushed, she started to feel the baby's head, so she quickly removed the sheet and said, "Okay, I think we got him!" She told me to push once more. This time, the baby's head emerged, and was completely out. She started to clean out his nose and mouth, then told me to pant so the rest of the body wouldn't come until she was ready.

The doctor said, "Okay, Patty, I'm ready. Let's get the baby completely out."

I pushed, and within seconds, the baby was out in the doctor's arms.

"It's a boy!" she said.

Tears and smiles filled the room. She called John and Sharon over. Sharon clamped the cord. The doctor wrapped the baby in a blanket and put him in Sharon's arms. I was so happy for them. John and I looked at one another, smiled, then looked over at the proud parents. In a little bit, we were both crying. Then *everyone* was crying—all except the baby! He was so content to be in his mother's arms, looking up at her. God, I can still feel that moment! It was so precious—I'll never forget it. I sat there watching the three of them together—it was beautiful. I was so thrilled to be able to make it happen for them.

Within minutes after the birth, Sharon told me she had been so afraid that she wouldn't feel like the mother. She said, "Patty, I feel so much like this baby's mom, you wouldn't believe it."

That made me feel good and also relieved, to know Sharon felt like his mother, and to hear her say it. To me, she was always the mother, right from the day of conception. I told her, "Sharon, I'm so glad you feel that way because I *don't* feel like this baby's mom. He's *your* son!"

Everyone left the birthing room except the parents, their son, and John and I. They left us alone for about an hour. Then we phoned my parents to tell them the baby was born and everyone was fine. Then the father called his parents to tell them they had a new grandson. While he was on the phone, he looked over at all of us and said, "I guess I can tell you all now—I really did want a son!"

As for Sharon, she couldn't take her eyes off her new little boy. She talked to him like you wouldn't believe—and couldn't stop kissing him. It was such a treat to sit there and watch!

Then Sharon brought the baby over to me so I could see him. He looked so much like his daddy! I have to admit I was curious when they told me he was a boy. When John and Michael were born, they looked exactly alike. I *did* wonder if he would look like my two sons. But when I looked at the baby, he had the same eyes, nose and mouth as his father—I was really glad he did.

After an hour or so, the nurse came in to tell us it was time for her to take the baby to the nursery. Sharon didn't want to leave him— she didn't even want him out of her arms. God had finally given her a son after ten years of trying. She handed the baby to the nurse, and walked over to me and my husband. She couldn't even say anything to us. She didn't need to—the look in her eyes said it all!

They walked out of the birthing room and, just as the door closed, it opened again—but only enough for Sharon's head to pop in. She just smiled at us, and then the door closed again.

20

Hospital Stay

I was overwhelmed—it was all over. Everything had gone great and I was feeling good. In fact, I didn't even feel like I had just given birth. I didn't need any stitches, which was nice. As far as the labor, I couldn't even say it was very hard.

My husband stayed with me a little longer. Right after the parents left, the nurse came in to tell us the baby's weight—7 lbs., 14 oz. My husband and I looked at each other, amazed—that was exactly what our first son weighed.

I told John he had better go home and get some sleep because I was going up to my room shortly also to get some rest. I ended up staying in the birthing room for about an hour after John left. I was glad to have some time alone. I sat there, thinking about everything.

I had wondered how I would feel after I gave birth to this very special baby. When I was pregnant, I always got the same question from *everyone*—"How will you be able to give up the baby?"

Well, I can honestly say I felt exactly like I knew I would. I felt very fortunate that, after the birth of the baby, I really felt the baby belonged to John and Sharon. Believe me, I was the happiest woman on earth and to have had them with me during the birth made things even better. I know not everyone can understand that, but if John and Sharon did, that was all I needed to make me happy.

I didn't need approval for what I did from anyone, except my husband John, Sharon and her John, and God. Most of all, I needed to know in my heart, that I did the right thing and this I was certain of. I thanked God for giving me the chance to be a Surrogate Mother.

As I was thinking all this, in came the nurse to take me to my room. It was nice to get settled in, take a shower, have something to eat, and finally fall asleep.

They woke me up for lunch. Just as I finished eating, Susan—who was in charge of the maternity unit—walked in to talk with me. She was the one who had made it possible for John and Sharon to have their own private room at feeding time. She told me it was all right if I wanted to spend some time alone with the baby to say goodbye, and went on to say that most mothers like to say goodbye to their babies before they put them up for adoption.

Boy, did that sound strange to my ears. I never thought of the baby as ever really being mine. To me, the adoption was only the legal procedure we had to go through and a lot of unnecessary paperwork. As far as I was concerned, the baby was always John and Sharon's son. Therefore, the adoption, in my eyes, never had to take place.

When you put a baby up for adoption, it is going to two people who are strangers. This child was going to his real father and his wife—a woman who wanted this baby so much, that she was willing to let another woman carry the baby for her. *That's* his real mom! Do you hear me, Patty? Susan was still talking to me but I couldn't give her my full attention. I was too absorbed in my own thoughts.

After Susan left, I gave her suggestion some thought. After lunch, I walked down to the nursery. Looking in the window, I saw all the babies sleeping. Then I saw the baby I had just delivered a few hours ago. He looked so precious, sound asleep. Since John and Sharon had gone home, I thought about feeding him, instead of having a nurse feed him. I asked the nurse if she could bring the baby to my room for the next feeding.

An hour or so before the feeding time, I started to get second thoughts. Did I have the right to ask to feed Sharon's son? Shouldn't I call and ask her permission first? Too late—I heard all the babies coming down the hall!

The nurse brought him in and left him by my bedside and believe it or not, I didn't know what to do. First, I just sat there on the edge of the bed staring at him. He was sound asleep, and did he look precious! I didn't have the heart to wake him up. I sat there, waiting for him to wake up by himself, then realized that maybe he wouldn't. So I picked him up and got the bottle ready—that was another story! I never did bottle-feed my own babies. I finally got comfortable on the bed, with him in my arms. Then, he tried to open his eyes and wake up. I sat there, just staring at him. I smiled, and as he opened his eyes, he smiled back. I think we sat there for what seemed like hours. I felt that he and I were very special friends.

I told him how lucky he was to have two very special parents, and how much they loved him. How proud I was to have helped at his birth. I would never forget him—I wanted him to know that! After I fed him, the nurse took him back to the nursery. As they left, the phone rang. It was Sharon asking about her son. I told her I had just fed him, and she said that was fine. She was pleased to hear that he drank his bottle. As I hung up, I wondered if I would see the three of them together before we all left the hospital. I hoped they would feed him in my room so I could witness that. It's strange, the whole time I was pregnant, I visualized how the birth and hospital stay would go. So far, everything was happening just as I had hoped.

Just then, my mother and father walked in. I knew they wanted to see the baby, so I asked them if they wanted to walk down to the nursery.

"Of course," they said, and the three of us walked down there.

I'm still not sure exactly how my parents felt when they saw the baby. My mom said he looked like John and Michael, but I told her, "Mom, if you could see his dad—he looks exactly like him." I really didn't think he looked like my sons, just a little resemblance. But all babies do look like one another to some degree.

I didn't expect anyone else to come visit me, since the baby wasn't mine. But someone did —an intern at the hospital, who had just heard about the birth. He had come in to tell me how special he thought I was to have done that for someone else.

At dinnertime, the phone rang again. This time, it was one of my aunts. It was nice to hear from her and in fact, she had called a few times while I was in the hospital. I never knew how she felt about me being a Surrogate. During my pregnancy, she never talked about it with me. I was just glad she called to talk and to see how I was feeling.

First thing the next morning, the lawyer came to see the baby. It was only 7:00 a.m. I was glad I had gotten up early enough to shower and get dressed before he arrived. I saw him down by the nursery window looking at the babies, so I walked down to say hello. I couldn't believe what he said to me—when he looked at my belly, he asked me if I was still pregnant! I only laughed, and so did he. What else could I do? I'm sure you all know what I *felt* like doing!

After he left the hospital, I went back to my room and had breakfast. About 9:00 a.m. I looked over at the door and saw flowers coming in—with Sharon carrying them. Boy, were they gorgeous! The thought that John and Sharon even bought them for me made me want to cry.

It was then I told Sharon if they wanted to feed the baby in my room, I would love to have them. So, they went to get the baby and brought him back to my room. It was so great to sit there watching them change him, feed him, and make such a fuss over him.

All Sharon kept saying to me was, "Patty, are you sure you don't mind us in your room?"

"Not at all, just seeing you together with your son makes the past nine months all worth it!" I was just glad John and Sharon felt comfortable enough to be around me with their baby.

That was the morning feeding. After the baby went back to the nursery, John and Sharon left the hospital saying they would be back in the afternoon to feed the baby again. And within hours, they were back in my room again. I sat there amazed how everything was going just as I had hoped—the joy I felt you can't imagine! When the baby went back to the nursery, John and Sharon said goodbye. They would see me in the morning—when we were all going home. I wondered what would happen then. With other Surrogates, the lawyer is the one who hands the baby over to his new parents. I didn't want that to happen with us. I felt since I knew John and Sharon, *I* wanted to be the one to hand the baby to Sharon. It would be so impersonal to have the lawyer do it—I just wouldn't feel comfortable with that. Sharon called me later. We talked about it and she told me she wanted me to be the one to hand her the baby. I was so glad and so relieved that Sharon felt the same way I did.

After I had dinner that night, my mother-in-law called to see how I was. I told her how much I missed the boys and she asked if it was all right to bring them up to the hospital to visit me. The nurses said it was fine, so at 7:00 p.m. I met them as they got off the elevator. God, did they look cute! They both had the same outfits on, which their Mom-Mom had just bought them. They had a lot of hugs and kisses for me, but I had even more for them! They kept asking me when I was coming home. I told them in the morning as soon as Daddy picked me up, we would be over to pick them up.

We went to the nursery so I could show them the baby. One of the nurses held him up at the window, so they could see him. I don't really think they fully understood what had happened, because my two-year-old kept touching my belly and saying the baby was still in there.

It was really hard to say goodbye to the boys—they kept crying and wanting me to go with them. Finally, they took their Mom-Mom's hands. I stood by the nursery watching them as they disappeared into the elevator.

Before I went back to my room, I stood by the nursery window looking in at the baby. I don't remember exactly how long I stood there. I was thinking how happy I was feeling for John and Sharon and wondering if other Surrogates felt the same way after they gave birth. As I walked away, I realized I had tears in my eyes. Everything was blurred as I walked into my room. I sat on the edge of the bed and cried—for John, Sharon, and their newborn son. I had no regrets, and I knew that never in my life would I regret what I had just done.

I was getting ready for bed when one of the nurses from the nursery walked in. I looked at her and thought, what's wrong? She explained that the nursery was really busy. There was no one to feed the baby. Would I mind if he came into my room for his feeding? What could I say, except okay? Besides, it would be nice to spend a little more time with him. I would probably never see him again, so I told her, "Sure, I'd love to feed him for you."

An hour later, in he came! This time, he was wide awake. I changed him, talked to him a while, then I fed him. It was really nice to have this time with him alone. In fact, the nurses never came in to get him. When he finally went to sleep, I put him in the cradle and stared at him. I sat there for an hour or so, just watching him sleep, then I wheeled him back to the nursery. Before the nurses came out into the hall to take him, I bent down and kissed his forehead and made sure his blanket was tucked in nice and tight for the night.

As I walked back to my room, I thought about the morning, when we would all be leaving, me to go home to my family and the baby to go home to his family.

21

Saying Goodbye

At 10:00 a.m., my husband came to the hospital. The parents were already there, but they were in the nursery, giving their son a bath. When they got to the hospital, they brought the baby's bag into my room, and decided to dress him there.

My husband and I waited in my room for the parents and also for the discharge papers. John and Sharon came into the room with the baby. It was great to watch the two of them dressing him. They both dressed him, and they must have tried three different outfits on him! We were all laughing. One outfit was too big. Another was a little too long. My husband and I just sat there watching two very proud parents getting their son ready to take home.

The father then said, "Why don't we just put his undershirt on with his diaper?"

It was summertime and it was a gorgeous day so the baby really didn't need any more than that but Sharon continued to dress him. Oh no—here come the hats! The first hat was too big—we all burst into laughter. The next hat looked just right. Boy, did he look adorable! In fact, all three of them looked perfect together. I couldn't help but get a big smile on my face and to shed a tear. I really wanted to cry, but I didn't want John and Sharon to misunderstand the reason for my tears. Besides, I promised myself I wouldn't cry when I said goodbye to John, Sharon and the baby. I didn't want to upset them. After all, the day they took their newborn son home was probably the biggest day in their life.

I had no regrets at all. To tell you the truth, this was one of the biggest days in *my* life, too. If I did end up shedding any tears, they would have been for their happiness, nothing else.

Now, everyone was ready to leave the hospital—we just had to wait for the discharge papers. My husband and I walked down to the nurse's station to see what the holdup was. The nurses were waiting to get some test results they had done on the baby that morning, because he had a little jaundice. The nurses made a few phone calls and soon we got the word we could all leave. They told us the baby would have to be seen by a doctor after he got home to check the jaundice. No problem—Sharon had already made an appointment with her pediatrician.

Our husbands took some things down to the cars. Just as we were ready to leave, the nurse came in and handed me the hospital papers— with the baby's footprints! She had made two copies, one for Sharon and also one for me. I thought that was really nice of her. I'm glad I got to keep a copy for the remembrance of this very special occasion.

We all walked out of the room together. One of the nurses had to carry the baby downstairs to the cashier while we checked out. Then, the nurse was ready to hand the baby to his mother. I turned around and everyone was just standing around waiting.

The nurse looked at me, seeming to feel a little awkward. She said, "Who should I hand the baby to?"

I just answered, "His mother, of course."

So she walked over to Sharon and handed the baby to her. He was all wrapped up in an adorable blanket that Sharon had gotten for him. The nurse said, "It was really nice to get to know all of you. I wish you all the luck in the world with your new son." She then said goodbye and left to go back upstairs.

We then went outside, the sun was shining. It was *such* a beautiful day! The five of us ended up walking down Vine Street together, as our cars were both parked down on Fifteenth Street. Deep down, I was glad we still had a few more minutes together. I was going to miss seeing and talking with Sharon and her husband. It was a little awkward to walk down the street together but I was glad that's how it turned out.

Halfway down the street, my husband looked at me. It was time to say goodbye. I really didn't want to—I had grown so fond of Sharon in those nine months. I felt I was losing a special friend. I wasn't sure how to go about saying goodbye. I just knew I didn't want to cry! I was feeling much too happy.

Right then, my husband said, "Well, I think we'd better get going."

We all stopped and looked at one another. My husband said goodbye first, and wished them both all the happiness in the world with their new son. I was nervous about saying goodbye because I was afraid it would make me cry! But I knew I couldn't put it off any longer—the time to say goodbye had finally come. I walked over, kissed the baby, and said goodbye to him. Then I looked up at Sharon— gave her a big kiss and hug, and wished her all the best. Then I walked over to her husband, John. Mind you, I was still under control at this point. But when I went to hug him and say goodbye, I saw tears in his eyes. That did it! I gave him a big hug, and started to cry—*hard*.

He said, "Thanks, Patty, for everything you did for us."

I couldn't stop crying. My husband put his arm around me, and we walked toward our car. We watched the three of them get into their car, then headed toward my mother-in-law's house to pick up the boys. The tears just wouldn't stop! On the way there, all I thought about was how happy John, Sharon and the baby were going to be.

As we parked the car at my mother-in-law's, John and Michael came running into my arms. I had to try to forget everything but my two sons! How happy I was to be their mom, and to finally be home with them!

22

Moving On

A few days after I came home from the hospital, my mother and father called and said they wanted to talk to me. They heard I was going to visit Ryan and Mary, but wanted to see me before I went to their house.

I went to my parents' house and they told me what had happened. It turned out Ryan and Mary were pretty upset about the fact that my parents came to the hospital to see me when I had the baby. They had a big fight with my parents and were not speaking to them because of me. For that reason, my parents thought it best if I didn't go to see them. I didn't agree with them—Ryan and Mary had told me in the very beginning they thought it was great I was being a Surrogate Mother.

So regardless of what my parents told me, I went to their house. Everything went fine until I talked with Ryan. One thing led to another. He said that my parents should never have come to the hospital to see the baby I sold.

I tried to tell him that my parents came to see *me*—their daughter.

He said, "Who are you kidding? They came to see the baby!"

The fact that I got money really bothered them. I couldn't understand that. From the start, they were all for Surrogate Mothering, until I actually had the baby and got the money.

As we talked about it, I finally realized why they were so upset. When they had their first son, my parents didn't go to the hospital to see him and the fact that they came to see me— and the baby that wasn't even mine—really bothered them.

I tried to explain that when they had their son it was in the dead of winter and we just had a bad snow storm. I reminded Ryan that

Dad doesn't even like to drive in the rain, let alone snow, so he should try to understand the reason why they didn't come to the hospital. Then I said, "If you remember, the day Mary came home with the baby Mom and Dad were right there at the house to see them. Besides, Mom and Dad tried to get a bus to the hospital but no buses were running because of the snow and ice."

Ryan just said he didn't want to hear any excuses so I dropped the subject and hoped that someday he would realize how much my parents love him and his family regardless of their actions. I know today, if Ryan had another child, my parents would get to the hospital no matter what—even if they had to go by dogsled! Now my parents know how important it is to Ryan and Mary and what it means to them. Some things in life are just more important to some people than to others and we all have to learn to respect that. After we dropped the subject, things cooled down and the rest of the visit was fine.

As it turned out, it seems like the whole thing blew over, because they never bring up the fact I was a Surrogate.

A few days after the episode, I got a call from one of my brothers. He was the one who thought that the whole thing was immoral and didn't talk about the pregnancy the entire nine months.

He said he just finished reading an article in the paper on the birth of John and Sharon's son. He thought the story was very touching, and he *did* think it was a nice thing I did for them.

Here's the article that appeared in the local newspaper about two weeks after the birth took place. The headlines read:

IT'S A BOY! CHILDLESS COUPLE HELPS DELIVER SON BORNE BY SURROGATE MOTHER!

Pat woke up with labor pains at about 1:30 a.m. Miles away, at about the same time, Sharon inexplicably woke up. A few hours later, the two women and their husbands were in the birthing room at Hahnemann University Hospital in Philadelphia.

There, Pat gave birth to a son. Sharon clamped the baby's umbilical cord, and the child was placed in her arms.

It was the culmination of eleven years of trying to have a child for Sharon and her husband John. And for Pat, a 30-year-old Burlington County woman, it was the culmination of a longtime desire to share with a childless couple the joy she's gotten from her own two sons.

Pat is a Surrogate Mother. She was artificially inseminated with John's sperm and was paid $15,000 to have the baby for John and Sharon. But she said she wanted to be a Surrogate, even before she knew money was involved.

"I can't have children," Sharon said in a telephone interview yesterday, just a week and a half after her son's June 21st birth. "I have been through operations—there is so much scar tissue now. The more they do, the more I scar."

She and John have been trying since the third year of their thirteen year marriage to have children. They thought about adoption, Sharon said, but the children that are available for adoption wouldn't be readily accepted by their neighbors. "We would accept them," she said, "but it wouldn't be fair to them. We talked to doctors, and they said to bring a child from a different background into this area would be very unfair."

About two years ago, they heard about Surrogate Mothering and contacted a place in California that referred them to Surrogate Mothering Ltd. in Philadelphia, a service that opened in 1981.

Meanwhile, Pat had learned about a Surrogate Mothering program in Kentucky and decided to apply. Before she became involved, however, she found herself pregnant with her second son, now two years old. After the baby's birth, she again looked into becoming a Surrogate Mother.

Sharon and John chose her to be the Surrogate Mother of their child. All the legalities were worked out, and attempts at artificially inseminating Pat with John's sperm began.

Pat said her own husband supported her decision. After five tries, Pat became pregnant. "It was like he was telling me a friend who had been trying for ten years got pregnant, and I felt so happy for her," Pat said.

"I cried," said Sharon, remembering when she learned Patty was pregnant. "My husband and I both cried."

Patty wrote to Sharon and John through the lawyers and told them she would like them to be present at the birth. "I feel that it is her baby, and I want her to be as much a part of it as possible," Patty said in an interview before the birth.

Throughout the pregnancy, the women kept in touch. Patty would tell Sharon how she was feeling, and Sharon would tell Patty about the preparations she and her husband were making for the baby.

They both thought the child would be a boy, but Sharon picked out a girl's name too, "just in case."

In the beginning, Sharon was afraid Patty might want to keep the baby. "But the more I talked to Patty, I felt she had no intention of keeping this baby," Sharon said. "And I worried so much about her."

At about 2:30 a.m. on June 21st, when Patty definitely knew she was going to the hospital, she called Sharon, who told her she already had been awake. From 5:00 a.m. until 6:45 a.m. when John the Third was born, Sharon and John were with Patty and her husband in the birthing room.

The baby weighed 7 lbs. 14 oz. and was 21 inches long. With the birth of her other two sons, Patty said she was "just anxious to see them for myself. I couldn't wait to see "my" baby." But with this child, she said, "I was just anxious for the baby to come out and go to the parents and to see how they were going to act."

She said she had some apprehension that the child might look like her other two sons, but he didn't. He looked just like his father, she said.

"The mother clamped the cord, and the doctor handed the baby right to Sharon," Pat said. "We were all crying, and it was really nice. The mother just kept on talking to the baby and kissing him."

"It was fantastic," Sharon said, "watching my baby being born. When they handed me this baby, and I clamped the cord, that baby was mine from the time he was put into my arms. Words can't describe what I feel for Patty," she said, and to Pat, also, the experience was special.

"Giving birth to my own sons was really a

beautiful experience," she said, "but never like this. I guess to be able to make two people happy and to share in their happiness for those three days, (the days in the hospital) made it all the more special."

Sharon plans to tell her son the circumstances of his birth when he is old enough to understand ... to tell him how wanted he was and that his biological mother "was a great person that she did this."

Patty said she and her husband don't want any more children, but if John and Sharon want another child, she would be a Surrogate Mother again for them. Sharons thinks having a brother or sister for John would be "wonderful." But for now, she said, "I think I will spoil this one for a while."

I was real pleased with the article, since it changed my brother's mind about me being a Surrogate.

The weekend after I got home from the hospital we moved out of our apartment. We rented a U-Haul and some of our close friends came over to help load the truck, along with my uncle and cousin's husband. We were taking everything down to our new house and storing it in the basement until the upstairs was completed. The house was still under construction so Michael and I were going to stay with my parents for a month or so. But, this weekend we were all going to Virginia to unload our belongings.

While the guys loaded up the truck, we girls sat out back talking. It was then I realized how concerned my girlfriends had been about me being a Surrogate Mother.

That night, after everyone left, I was happy to get some sleep. I was anxious to see the house again but somewhat sad that, after the weekend, big John and little John would be staying to finish the house, while Michael and I would be going home to my mom's. I was still working full time and, to tell you the truth, I'm not one for roughing it!

It took almost two months to complete the house. I tried to go down every other weekend with Michael. That was really hard because I worked all day Friday and had to go back to work Monday morning. I didn't mind the four-hour drive at all. I just didn't like getting there Saturday morning, turning around and coming right back home on Sunday, especially after not seeing my husband and oldest son for two weeks. After doing that a few times, we finally decided it was too important for our family to be together. My place was with my husband, even if I did have to rough it for a while. I went into work and gave my two-week notice. Actually, I gave my boss a month's notice, so he would have time to find another girl for me to train before I left.

My husband promised me he would try and have the bathroom hooked up by the time Michael and I arrived.

Two months of staying with my mom and dad really made our relationship closer. I was really grateful for the time I spent with them. We spent a great deal of time sitting in their kitchen, talking. Some nights we sat there until 2:00 a.m. I got to know them better than I ever had before. It was great!

One night, I went over to my aunt's house to visit. When I came back, my parents told me Sharon had called and said she would call back later. I couldn't wait!

Right after the birth, when everybody was back home, I wondered about Sharon and how she was doing at being a "mom". I hoped it was just like she had dreamed about. For me, it would be nice to hear it from her.

My parents started to tell me they had had a nice conversation with Sharon when she called. I was curious as to what they said. I surely didn't want them to say anything to upset her. As my dad started to tell me, I saw tears in my mom's eyes. My dad tried to explain to me how very proud he was of me for doing what I did for John and Sharon. Just from talking with her, they could tell how happy she was with her new son.

Then my mom said, "You know, Patty, I really wish we could have met John and Sharon. I would have really liked that."

Then I realized they had been hoping to run into John and Sharon the day they came to the hospital. I told my parents all I could about them and what kind of people they were. I think that helped some.

When Sharon called back, the first thing she said was, "I hope I didn't upset your parents."

I said, "No, Sharon, not at all. They are really happy for you both." I told her if there was ever a time she needed me for anything—anything at all—I hoped she would get in touch with me, and not to hesitate for a second!

Before I could continue, Sharon asked, "Patty, how are *you*? Are you O.K.?"

Whenever Sharon calls, she is always concerned with my feelings and how I'm handling things now that the birth is over. I always try my best to let her know I have no regrets—and more than anything I feel the baby I delivered is *her* son!

She told me how much she loved her son and loved being a mom. She wanted to do so many things with him. She told me she didn't even mind when he woke her up at 2 a.m. and couldn't get back to sleep. She loved every minute of holding and walking him until he finally fell back to sleep. At times, she said, she thought the carpet would wear out!

I've heard a lot of new mothers talk about their newborns but Sharon—she beat them all! She still couldn't believe she was a mom—until she realized how often she was walking the floor in the middle of the night, holding her precious bundle of joy.

The following Friday was my last day at work. I had trained a new girl and she was enjoying the work and doing well at her job. The only thing I was going to miss was the money. But I knew the feeling would leave me after I got down to the new house and my family. I was going to start my own business. I was looking forward to that! I was going to open a beauty salon in our home.

The Friday night before Michael and I left for Virginia, my parents took us out to dinner. When we got back to my mom's, I got Michael ready for bed and tucked him in for the night. I ended up sitting in the kitchen with my parents till way past midnight. It would be our last night together for some time. They had promised to come visit us once a month, except in the wintertime when there was snow or ice.

By 10:00 a.m. the next morning, Michael and I were on our way to Virginia. When we drove up our driveway, what a beautiful feeling! The house looked great, even though it was not finished inside yet. We had temporary electricity and the plumbing was still not completed. We did have a well, but no running water. Our refrigerator and stove were hooked up, so at least we could cook our meals in the house.

It was a little tough for me in the beginning. Believe me, though, it was great for our family to be together! However, there were times I couldn't believe I had moved down before the house was completed. One day I got so upset with all the dirt all over the floors that I started sweeping like a crazy person! Dust and dirt was flying all over but I didn't care—I had to get the place clean. John walked in and tried to explain that, no matter how much I swept, it wouldn't help until the sanding of the drywall was finished. I think he realized how upset I was because he suggested we go back to New Jersey to visit our families. That way, Don, a friend of ours, could come in and finish taping and sanding the drywall and when we got back the walls would be ready for us to paint. Boy, did I feel better!

After we got back, it was only a matter of a few weeks before the painting was finished, and the bathrooms were hooked up. Little by little, everything else was completed.

Now it was the end of August. John and I had to go back to Philadelphia to go to court. We had to give up our parental rights to John and Sharon's baby. That sounded weird to me, but it was something that had to be done for the courts.

The entire time we sat in the courtroom, it seemed like a dream. I remember sitting there wondering why on earth I was there. In my heart, I didn't need to tell any judge that I was giving up my rights—to me, I had none to give up from the beginning. I also felt that there was no need for an adoption, because John and Sharon were the legal mother and father from the day of conception. So when I had to go in front of the judge and answer all those questions, I felt it was just a procedure that wasn't necessary in our case.

With some Surrogate Mothers, you need to do all that, I guess. But I knew how *I* felt, as well as how John and Sharon felt. We all knew who that little guy belonged to.

The judge then started asking my husband questions about him giving up his parental rights. Now, that was *really* bizarre! I felt—God, my husband didn't have any rights at all, any more than I did! When we finished signing the papers, the lawyers shook our hands and said goodbye. We walked out. Boy, were we glad to be out of the courtroom and on our way home!

23

Contract Disputes

About six months after the birth of John and Sharon's son, I went down to our mailbox to pick up our mail. When I opened the box, there was a letter from Sharon! I had talked with her on the phone a few times. I also received a Christmas card from her family, but today there was a thick envelope. When I first looked at it, I thought maybe Sharon had enclosed some pictures of the baby. I couldn't wait to open it. When I did, I couldn't believe what I was reading.

Sharon explained in the letter she would understand if I didn't want to get involved. She went on to tell me about the bill she received from the lawyers. She had no one to talk to about it but me.

Sharon had requested an itemized bill from the lawyer, because her attorney who was handling the final adoption needed the bill to present in court. Usually, the lawyers in the program handle the whole adoption procedure but John and Sharon had wanted their own lawyer to handle theirs because they lived in another county. In most cases the lawyers in the program handle the adoption so the adoptive couple has no reason to request an itemized bill, therefore they never actually see the charges.

Sharon had requested an itemized bill from the lawyer, because her attorney who was handling the final adoption needed the bill to present in court. Usually, the lawyers in the program handle the whole adoption procedure but John and Sharon had wanted their own lawyer to handle theirs because they lived in another county. In most cases the lawyers in the program handle the adoption so the adoptive couple has no reason to request an itemized bill, therefore they never actually see the charges.

Most couples are satisfied with paying the lawyers and letting them handle all the bills.

They don't even ask to see any of the bills. All they know is they pay the lawyers somewhere around $10,000, which is good enough for them. I think if they asked for an itemized bill, they might have some questions about where all that money is going.

Well, Sharon said the lawyer took a long time to send her the bill, and only finally sent it because their attorney kept calling, telling him that he needed the bill for the adoption. So, after months of asking, Sharon finally received the itemized bill.

Some of the expenses were easy to understand. Then there were some that were outrageous—like the fee for the psychologist. In the contract that was signed by all of us, it stated that I had the option of going every week to see the psychologist if I felt I needed to, or if *he* thought I needed to. But, I was only required to go once in the beginning of the program for the initial visit. As it turned out, I only went once—for about ninety minutes. You'll never guess what the fee was for that one visit—would you believe $2,100! Now *really*, what doctor has the right to charge that amount? Especially for a ninety minute session.

At first, I thought the medical doctor was also charging too much, but I have a girl-friend who is in the process of being inseminated with her husband's sperm. That doctor is charging her $300 per visit. So the physician's fee came pretty close to the amount the doctor charged Sharon. What I didn't like was his attitude when Sharon requested the bill. He sent a letter to the lawyer, with a copy to Sharon. I felt it was very unprofessional. I'd like to share part of that letter with you:

"It is not possible for me to offer an itemized bill because my fee in this matter does not reflect specific items of care but rather an overall fee for all the care in which I did provide. I do not keep track of the number of visits as that is of no consequence as far as I am concerned. In essence, this is the same as if I were operating on a patient. I charge a flat fee for a given operation, whether it is an easy or difficult case and whether the patient required short- or long-term postoperative care. The fee is the same. (That's hard for me to believe.)

My fee in this instance not only involves the actual insemination and monitoring of the Surrogate, but all the visits prior to the actual selection, the monitoring of her menstrual cycles to determine the proper day of ovulation, etc., etc.

The best response I can give in this instance concerns the following anecdote. A gentleman was having trouble with his plumbing and called a plumber. The plumber came to the man's house, looked around, and banged on the man's pipes. He then sent a bill for $50. The man thought this bill was excessive and demanded an itemized bill from the plumber. The plumber returned an itemized bill with the following notation. 'For banging on your pipes—$5.00. For knowing where to bang—$45.00.' In essence, I feel that my fee reflects as much 'knowing where to bang' as anything else. It is not a fee for a specific number of visits. My fee would be essentially the same if the Surrogate had taken longer to conceive or if she had conceived in the first cycle. I believe it is a fair fee, reflecting not only the services performed, but also the knowledge and expertise required to perform those services.

I also resent the issue being raised at this time. I believe that you fully explained the fee schedule to the parents prior to their entrance into our program and they were all too willing to pay those fees at that time. Now when they have a baby, the situation has turned around. I think it unfair of them to now try to evade payment . . .''

I couldn't believe he wrote that letter.

Another fee on the itemized bill which completely floored me was the fee for "flowers". When I was in the hospital, I got a bouquet of flowers from the lawyer, medical doctor and also the psychologist. At least, that is what the card said. I thought it was so nice of them all to send me flowers. I called each one of them personally and thanked them. I found out later the three of them had the nerve to send the bill to John and Sharon! I feel if they were sending the bill to the couple, they should have signed the card, "the adoptive couple", or something to that effect. I just couldn't believe the three of them couldn't have chipped in and paid for the flowers out of their own money!

Sharon had told me the psychologist was sending her an itemized statement for his bill. As of today, one year later, she is still waiting. She was told he was out of the office, due to illness. I told Sharon he probably got sick the day he opened his mail and found the request for the bill for $2,100!

One reason why I think the lawyers don't like the couple and their Surrogate to meet is for this reason—having them go over the bills together. I'm sure if Sharon had never met me and had received the bill for $2,100, she simply would have assumed I went to him throughout the pregnancy, and thought nothing of it.

I think some lawyers and doctors feel the couple want children so much, they will pay any price and not question their fees at all.

In the beginning, the couple put the lawyer's fee in escrow. After the baby is born and the bills are paid, the lawyers reimburse the couple for any money which is left. In most cases, the couple does receive some money back. This makes me feel that the couple just thinks, "Well, it didn't cost as much as we thought—good!" Little do they know—it probably wouldn't have cost them the original $10,000 to start with!

The last time I spoke with Sharon in March, the adoption still wasn't final—because of the itemized bill and the fees in question. Sharon did tell me that she was hoping they could celebrate two things in June—their son's first birthday and also the final adoption.

One thing I know for sure—John and Sharon waited ten years for their son. He means the world to them! And I am so happy I was able to share in something as special as their son's birth.

24

One Year Later

We're pretty much settled in our new home now. I can't tell you how much I love it! The house still needs some things done, but nothing I can't live without—things like interior doors, the kitchen countertop, and window trim.

We opened a beauty salon, John Michael's, in our home and the shop is doing extremely well. I love having our own business right in our home. It will especially be nice having the shop downstairs when the baby comes along. That's right—you guessed it! Our two sons are about to have a new brother or sister. I got pregnant five months after I delivered John and Sharon's son. No, it wasn't planned at all. In fact, it was a shock! But we are looking forward to his arrival in about a week.

We had an ultrasound done and guess what! It's going to be another boy. Can you believe it, three boys! How do I tell my mom? She will truly be disappointed but John and I aren't. We love having boys.

I hear from Sharon now and then. The three of them are doing just great. She tells me her son is the best thing that has ever happened to her. I genuinely enjoy getting letters and phone calls from her. I am so glad we have that special "bond" between us.

I think of Sharon a lot. In the little time I got to know her, I grew so very fond of her. I believe there will always be a bond between us. I hope she knows that she and her family have a very special place in my heart. I thank God for giving me the opportunity to help John and Sharon bring their son into the world.

I do have to admit though, come June, I will think about John and Sharon and the baby's birth. I do love that little guy—in a "special" way. It isn't the way I love my own sons, since, after all, he really isn't my son. The love I have for my own children grows every day, simply because I am with them all the time, and they are part of my life. The love I have for John and Sharon's son is because I shared nine months of my life with him and helped bring him into the world.

When he gets old enough to understand, I hope he will realize just how lucky he is that his parents found someone like me to help bring him into this world. I hope he also realizes he has a very "special" place in my heart forever.

I often wonder what he looks like. It would be nice to get a picture of him, when Sharon sends me a letter. I guess that is my curiosity. Sharon tells me things about him—what he looks like—and how happy she is. On his first birthday, I stood in the store looking at the birthday cards for 1-year-olds and got this big smile on my face. I thought about Sharon and what she was doing that day with her son. I could imagine the party and all his gifts! Several weeks after his birthday, I did get a call from her. She told me all about the party she had for John. She even had a big bear for him—all dressed up! I just knew she would do something like that. When John gets older, he'll realize he's got the best mom in the world. I know that!

Our two sons never talk about the baby. Sometimes I think they were too young to understand just what I did. Who knows, when they get older, they may come to me and say, "Mom, remember when . . .?" I know, though, that when my husband and I feel John and Michael are old enough to understand, we will sit down with them and explain everything.

And, if any of you are still wondering, I have no regrets whatsoever. If John and Sharon called me tomorrow to ask me to be their Surrogate Mother again, I'd say, "Yes!" Of course, they would have to wait until after the birth of our third child. But, if they were willing to wait, I'd be willing to carry another baby for them.

25

From Family and Friends

I Am A Surrogate Grandfather

I can't forget the day my daughter informed me that she was going to be a Surrogate Mother. It was a moment of shock and disbelief.

I thought, *my* daughter—happily married with two beautiful sons—going to be a Surrogate Mother? *Why???*

My daughter then said to me, "I know how badly I wanted children, and I can understand how this woman feels. I thought I would be doing something really beautiful for this couple."

"Patty," I said, "you must be doing it for the money. After all, the fee you received is a lot of money."

"Dad," she replied, "I didn't even know about the money until after I decided to do it. Besides, I would do it for nothing just to help some couple have a child." Well, I could believe this, because my daughter is a beautiful person and would do something like this.

I still didn't accept it until she appeared on a television talk show about Surrogate Mothering. I thought the people in the audience were going to rake her over the coals. Was I ever wrong! My daughter handled herself very well. I think she convinced some of the audience that she was doing a good thing. She also convinced *me* at that point and I finally accepted it.

The months went by quickly. I thought, do I want to go see this baby when it is born? Well, the day came. Yes, my wife and I both went to the hospital to see our daughter and the beautiful little boy whom we would never see again.

I did feel a certain attachment for this child because he was part of my daughter but I also felt happiness for the couple who were going to get this precious little boy to raise and call their own.

My daughter is now pregnant with her third child. We are looking forward to another grandchild, but I will always care a little about her surrogate child. I will never forget our experience.

Ruth's Reaction

We ran into John and Patty in town the weekend they came down to Virginia to tell their friends about her pregnancy. They stopped briefly, but remained in the truck as we greeted each other and made arrangements to get together later in the afternoon at our house. Although the door was open on Patty's side, she was wearing a huge down jacket and I couldn't tell then she was pregnant. Looking back, I remember feeling it was odd that Patty didn't get out and hug me—she seemed constrained. We were occupied at the time with house hunting, however, and those feelings quickly passed.

Later, when Patty came in our front door, it was apparent at once that she was *very* pregnant. I was thrilled and immediately hoped she would have a girl. But before I could say two words, Patty said, "Look, it's not mine. I'm a Surrogate Mother. I'm having the baby for someone else."

I was puzzled, amazed, curious, excited, concerned and happy all at the same time. My concern stemmed only from my sense of Patty's uneasiness, but it evaporated as we talked and I realized she had been uneasy only over our reaction and not over the circumstances of the pregnancy.

Neither my husband John, nor I had any negative feelings about the pregnancy then or at any time. At the time, I was 38 and had given birth to my first child just a few months earlier. I had experienced my first physiological yearnings for children when I was 21. By the time my daughter was conceived, I had desired deeply to have a child for well over 12 years. Relationships had come and gone over the years, but I didn't find the man I wanted to marry until I was 35. In my early 30's, I went through a period of considering single parenthood—waiting was becoming *so* hard—but it seemed the right answer for me. I would have been devastated if, after waiting for so long, John and I had been unable to have children. I had no trouble at all relating to a couple who had tried for so many years only to find they couldn't have children. Had it been me, I would have been supremely grateful to a woman who could give of herself to give me a child of my own. All of these thoughts flowed through my mind as Patty talked.

For Patty herself, I felt the most profound respect and admiration that she would give of herself in this way. I realized she had given this decision years of thought and I never questioned it was the right decision for her.

Having had a difficult pregnancy and birth, I knew I would never *joyfully* do that for anyone! But I could understand that, having completed her own family (or so she thought), being in good health and enjoying being pregnant and giving birth, this seemed like a wonderful gift to give.

Patty was splendid that day—she seemed very calm, sure of herself and genuinely unattached to the child she carried. She said she never experienced the feeling that it was "her" child. She was blessed, I believe, for her selflessness by this sense of detachment. She seemed so noble—like a knight championing the cause of this childless couple.

Between her visit and the birth, I wondered if Patty would still feel detached if the baby was a girl, since she did not have a daughter of her own. Although she hadn't been worried about this possibility, I was relieved it was a boy. I called her the day she came home from the hospital and Patty described the development of her relationship with the baby's parents, the events surrounding the birth and her feelings as she saw and even held and fed the baby. It sounded so beautiful—filled with the purest kind of love—and I was awed by the enormity of what Patty had done and the strength of commitment and character by which she had kept the entire event on such a high plane of consciousness for everyone.

Patty's achievement seems even more impressive when viewed in light of the many negative reactions she received—from the coldly indifferent to the highly emotional to the downright hostile. She never seemed to waver in her belief that she was absolutely doing the right thing.

When I heard Patty was pregnant again with her own baby, I felt very happy about it. Somehow it seemed a very fitting thing that the last child would be her own. I knew then she would never have regrets.

Patty's Husband

Patty has been trying to get me to write something for the book for almost a year now. I have put it off for one reason or another, but now I've decided to write this especially for her.

It seems so long ago that it happened. I remember when Patty mentioned it. We were watching the news and that's when I first learned all about Surrogate Mothering. I didn't pay too much attention until I saw how serious she was.

While Patty was more into having the baby for the couple out of the goodness of her heart, I became interested because of the financial end of it. It seemed only right to me that Patty receive a fee for being a Surrogate Mother, as she would miss a certain amount of work and there *is* some risk to having a baby.

To my amazement, Patty was picked almost right away, but then I thought, why not? She is beautiful, healthy, and intelligent. She also had the perfect attitude to be a Surrogate Mother.

The inseminations started, but Patty had trouble getting pregnant right away. She went to the doctor's office many times.

I remember the day Patty came home and called to tell me she had seen John. I asked her at once what he looked like. Another time, she called to tell me she had met John and talked with him. Then I wanted to know what Patty thought about him—what kind of a guy he was and if he seemed nice. I was glad when Patty told me that she liked him very much.

Now Patty was pregnant and everybody was excited—me included! I was excited for John and Sharon, especially. It was really nice to share the whole pregnancy with them.

If anyone wants to ask, "Wasn't he jealous? How could he let his wife carry another man's baby?", my answer is that I never experienced any of those feelings. Patty and I love each other very much. We have a good relationship and I feel blessed to share my life with her. That's not to say there weren't a few times I'd wonder, "Is this right?"

As the pregnancy went on, Patty became

more excited about having John and Sharon's baby. I simply had to marvel at her. Her attitude was fantastic! I was happy when she started meeting with Sharon. I felt it was important for both of them. As the months went on, Patty's happiness increased, as did mine.

There was an incident when John (Sharon's husband) wanted to see Patty. He was in the area on business and called Patty to see if it was OK for them to meet. Patty called me at work to see how I felt about it. I thought sure, why not, after all, he *is* the expecting father. I thought it would be nice for him to see his child being carried. But after we hung up, a little jealousy set in. I thought, what is it with this guy, wanting to see MY wife—forgetting that it wasn't *my* wife he really wanted to see, but *his* baby. Later, I could feel how excited he must have been to actually see he was going to be a FATHER. I can honestly say that was my ONLY tough time, from the time we decided Patty was going to be a Surrogate, up to the actual delivery of the baby.

Another time I was concerned for Patty was when she was scheduled to appear on a television talk show. The boys and I dropped her off at the studio and drove on to my mother's to watch the show. As we watched, I thought the host was pretty rough on Patty.

I felt he asked a lot of negative questions but, as he told Patty after the show, viewers would want to know both sides. The people in the audience were mostly positive in their reactions. As I remember, there were maybe one or two people who thought Patty was doing a shocking thing. I can understand their feelings, but I don't believe they understood OUR feelings! When I picked Patty up at the studio after the show, she was radiant and very excited. She felt that the show went well and it didn't bother her how negative some of the people were towards her! Again, I marvelled at Patty.

I can understand that this issue is a very controversial subject. I can never hope to convince everybody that what we did was right. But the night we were all together in the birthing room and the baby was born, electricity filled the air. I remember John and Sharon's joyous tears when the baby was placed in their arms, as well as *our* tears for them. When John called his parents to tell them they had a grandson, there was not a dry eye in the room.

Two days later, when Patty and the baby were being released, we were all at the hospital. John and Sharon were in Patty's room dressing the baby. I think Sharon brought three outfits and I don't know how many hats for him. Sharon was so excited— she finally had her son! Saying goodbye was tough. We stood outside the hospital, crying and trying to think of the right thing to say. I realized at that point that we would never see these people again. We had come to love and respect them. And we were lucky to have shared in the most beautiful experience possible—the birth of their son.

26

Four Years Later

Much has happened recently with the Surrogate Mothering Program. It has been made illegal in the state of New Jersey where I originally grew up. It started last year when a surrogate mother decided to keep the baby she bore for an infertile couple. When that happened, it seemed like all one heard on the news reports was this story, and people formed their own opinions about the case and of Surrogate Mothering.

I remember the day when the court in Hackensack, New Jersey was making its decision as to who was to get custody of "Baby M." I flew to New York with Mark, my youngest son, to appear on the "Morning Program." As soon as I checked into our hotel, a limousine was waiting to drive us to the Hackensack courthouse. It was about an hour ride and when we arrived, I couldn't believe my eyes! People were everywhere—outside and inside the courthouse. We heard that some reporters had even camped out the night before. While there, I was interviewed by Channel 3 (a Philadelphia television station), and when I heard what the judge decided, I was very relieved. I was happy that the Sterns got custody of the child. I really believed all along that the Sterns would be the parents and not the woman who delivered that little girl. To me, a Surrogate Mother has no rights whatsoever to the baby.

When one decides to become a surrogate, that's exactly what one is—a surrogate to that child and *not* his mother. If it were not for the infertile couple, the surrogate mother would not be pregnant with that particular child. The surrogate mother must realize even before the baby is born that it isn't her baby. I truly believe that most surrogate mothers are like myself and not like Mary Beth Whitehead, who changed her mind. Most surrogate mothers enter the program to give the gift of life to a woman who cannot have children. In my case, Sharon had an emptiness in her life that I filled. One cannot imagine the joy I felt when I saw Sharon and her husband holding their son the very first time.

Since the Baby M case, I have done a lot of newspaper interviews and TV appearances. Most people have their own opinions of Surrogate Mothering and I truly respect how they feel about the subject. I only wish people could understand more fully how the infertile couple feels and how a woman feels who becomes a surrogate mother in order to help an infertile couple.

And I really don't think it is anyone's concern except the Surrogate Mother's and the couple's. If a woman wants to be a surrogate, I think she has that right. And, if an infertile couple wants to employ a woman for nine months to carry the husband's child, they should have that right.

I appeared on a television show, "People are Talking," in both Baltimore and Philadelphia in February, 1987. For the show in Philadelphia, Sharon and her son also appeared. It was an hour show, and I was excited to see Sharon again. I hadn't seen them since the birth and was really looking forward to seeing them again. I was curious to see John, too, to see how he had grown, to see Sharon and him together! While getting ready for the TV appearance that morning, I was really nervous and was glad my husband was there with me. We arrived at the studio and went into the "green room" to wait for Sharon. Within minutes she walked into the room. We embraced. God, it was good to see her! We were both in tears. Thank goodness we saw each other before the show to get our hellos in and our tears out of the way.

After the show we were able to spend a little time together. Sharon's sister took pictures and we got to talk with John. He talked more to my husband than he did to me, but I didn't mind. More than anything, I just wanted to see him with his mom. Believe me, he's adorable and very attached to Sharon.

In April I travelled to New York, California, Minnesota, and Washington. Mark—not quite two years old—went everywhere with me. He was still nursing and I couldn't leave him for more than a night. My husband, John, was great while I was away. I telephoned every night to ask how he and the boys were getting along.

The hardest trip was to California. I left on Sunday and was supposed to return the following Friday. But after a few days, I was ready to come home; I missed my family too much. My publisher was also in California. He met Mark and me at the airport and took us to our hotel. This was the first time I had ever been to the West Coast.

I was scheduled to do a talk show with Patty Duke. It was interesting to meet her since I watched her on "The Patty Duke Show" while I was growing up. She was very nice and I enjoyed appearing on her show. After that, I was scheduled to do a national television show at a studio across town. The timing was close but we made it with seconds to spare! I couldn't believe it—everyone seemed so calm when there were only seconds left.

On most of the shows, the guests included other surrogate mothers, attorneys, or those against surrogate mothering. Most of the time there were live audiences and I was always curious to find out how many people were for or against surrogate mothering.

One show in Minneapolis touched me deeply. Most of the audience were against surrogates. At the end of the show, a young woman in the audience stood up to tell her story. I was so glad she had the courage to share her story in front of everyone. She and her husband could not have children and they had tried over the years to adopt a child. She continued to say that adoption, in their case, was not especially easy. Her husband's job involved transfers, and every time they got settled in their new home they contacted an adoption agency. But when the agency found out about her husband's work, it continued to state that they did not have a stable home life for adoption. The couple turned to surrogate mothering. The one advantage is that they will now have a child that is biologically his.

While in California, I met with an agent, Mike. A friend from New Jersey had set up the meeting. We had lunch and talked about my book. He knew someone who might be interested in making my book into a movie. I was very excited. The next day, we met with the producer who had a positive attitude about the project. Although producers will probably want to do a movie about the Baby M case, mine is a more positive and happier story.

Being in California was nice but I felt lonely. I missed John and the boys something fierce. As the days went by, the more homesick I became and told Bill I had to leave. I called John and asked him to pick us up at the airport that very night! As the plane landed at Dulles Airport at about 10 p.m., I saw John and Michael standing at the windows. I couldn't wait to walk through the gates to get some hugs from John and the boys. It was a great welcome home!

I remember the first time I flew to New York. I was nervous because I had only been in a plane once before, when I was a teenager. I expected the plane to be huge and equipped with lots of seats. Well, when I boarded the plane I almost fainted. There were perhaps eighteen seats in the entire plane, and I couldn't even stand up straight. I walked toward the back of the plane to look for a little more room because Mark was with me. As the plane took off, I had to get my mind off flying. I believe the man sitting next to me could sense I was nervous because he started to tell me everything was going to be OK. Then, when he told me he had a gun and was going to hijack the plane, that was all I needed! Later I learned the man was an infamous '60s radical. As the plane landed, I thanked God and couldn't wait to get off and calm down.

My accommodations, provided by the television shows I was appearing on, were gorgeous. The hotel suite in Minneapolis was out of this world. As I walked into the living room with Mark and looked around, I wished my husband were there. There was a Jacuzzi and a bar area. I couldn't believe I was about to stay there for two nights with just my infant son and not my husband!

I really enjoyed appearing on the talk shows and telling my story. Even though I think Surrogate Mothering is a good alternative for infertile couples, I'll be the first to agree that

Surrogate Mothering isn't for everyone. All women cannot be surrogates and not all couples can handle the Surrogate Mothering process. But the couples who want to go that route should have every right to participate in the program.

When my hardcover publisher tried to get book signings at various bookstores, most were cancelled because the store managers were afraid of adverse public opinion.

In June, 1987, Sharon called and invited our family to meet hers in Ocean City, Maryland. We spent three days there. It was a beautiful time watching the boys play together. We went to the beach during the day and to the amusement park at night. While we were there we had a little birthday party for John, and the boys gave him presents. I really enjoyed seeing Sharon again and spending time with her. We even discussed the possibility of my having another child for her.

My boys are now eight, six, and almost three years old, respectively. We all went to Philadelphia recently to do another television show, "Time Out." As the boys sat in the audience, I don't think they fully understood what I did for Sharon and what it all means. They do talk freely about me being a Surrogate Mother and that I had a baby boy for Sharon; they tell their teachers when I go away to do television shows. Their teachers seem to think the boys are proud of their mom. Whether or not the boys really understand all this, I suppose I won't find out until they are somewhat older.

Once when I was going to speak at a nearby hospital on Surrogate Mothering to an infertility group, my six-year-old asked me where I was going and for what reason. I explained that I was going to talk to couples that couldn't have children. Do you know what he said? "Mom, are you going to have babies for all those couples, too?"

I have asked my sons how they would feel if I gave Sharon another baby so that John could have a brother or sister. It made me feel proud when they answered that it would be nice for John to have a brother or sister and nice for Sharon, too.

The last time I talked with Sharon I couldn't believe what happened. Several months ago, I decided to have my hair frosted. The stylist destroyed my hair and I had to have it cut short because she completely bleached my hair instead of frosting it. Because it was totally dried out, nothing could be done except to cut it. So I did. I told Sharon the story and she said the same thing had happened to her! I thought it was very interesting that both of us had the same experience with our hair at about the same time.

Now that it is approaching summer once

again, I wonder if we'll get together with Sharon and her family. I am so glad that we keep in touch and try to see one another every year. I never have had any regrets about being a Surrogate Mother for Sharon. It has full-filled Sharon's life and has given me an experience of unconditional love. It has also given Sharon and me a very special relationship and the chance, I believe, to feel true happiness in this lifetime.

☆　　☆　　☆

FREE!!
BOOKS BY MAIL
CATALOGUE

BOOKS BY MAIL will share with you our current bestselling books as well as hard to find specialty titles in areas that will match your interests. You will be updated on what's new in books at no cost to you. Just fill in the coupon below and discover the convenience of having books delivered to your home.

PLEASE ADD $1.00 TO COVER THE COST OF POSTAGE & HANDLING.

- -

BOOKS BY MAIL

320 Steelcase Road E.,
Markham, Ontario L3R 2M1

IN THE U.S. -
210 5th Ave., 7th Floor
New York, N.Y., 10010

Please send Books By Mail catalogue to:

Name _____
　　　　　　　　　　(please print)

Address _____

City _____

Prov./State _____ P.C./Zip _____

(BBM1)